THE LATE *Bloomer's* REVOLUTION

A Memoir

AMY COHEN

HYPERION
NEW YORK

Library of Congress Cataloging-in-Publication Data

Cohen, Amy

The late bloomer's revolution : a memoir / by Amy Cohen.

p. cm.

ISBN-13: 978-1-4013-0002-9

ISBN-10: 1-4013-0002-2

1. Cohen, Amy, 1966– 2. Television writers—United States—Biography. I. Title.

PN1992.4.C65A3 2007

808.2'25—dc22

[B] 2006049763

Design by Pauline Neuwirth, Neuwirth and Associates, Inc.

FIRST EDITION

10 9 8 7 6 5 4 3 2 1

This book is for my mother, the wonderful,
irreplaceable Joyce Arnoff Cohen

ACKNOWLEDGMENTS

THIS BOOK WOULD not have been even remotely possible if not for the following people. First, my father; a man who does not think twice at asking in a crowded elevator, "Ame, when's the last time you went to the gynecologist?" As you know, I just adore you. My incredible sister, swami, and constant rock, Holly Osman, for all the rah-rah, you can do it, it's good, keep writing, no you're not going crazy, honestly, crazy people never actually know they're going crazy—I think, anyway, you're just neurotic, incredibly, incredibly neurotic, in a loveable way—sort of, but you should really get out of the house—now, right now. Now! Okay, then, do you want me to come over? pep talks. You are just the best.

My family: Richard Osman, who endured my epic meltdown and random profanity the day he tried to teach me how to ride out of the Chase bank parking lot. My terrific, supportive, unpushy brother, Tommy Cohen, or as he likes to call himself "Formerly Chapter 24." The equally terrific Elisa Singer, Sarah and Eric Osman, Eli and Jessie Cohen, Aunt Betty Judson, and our favorite co-pilot, Beverly Albert.

My beloved, brilliantly funny Robin Swid, who listened to every line of every draft, and without whom this book would simply not exist. She gave her greatest performance every day, pretending she'd heard something for the first time, over and over again, and that it was good (when it wasn't).

The unsinkable Molly Friedrich, for believing even books can be Late Bloomers and for buying me an expensive dinner at Craftbar and getting me a little drunk when she didn't think I'd written a page. I cannot thank you enough. And for all their help: Paul Cirone, Andy "Later On" Marino, Nicole Kenealy, who should be considered for Sainthood, if only for listening to my long-winded computer questions.

At Hyperion, My Editor, the queen of the perfect one-liner, the great Brenda Copeland, who is so funny and quick that I'm having trouble thinking of something funny and quick enough to capture all her funny quickness. Kathleen "Rock Star Supernova" Carr. The unbelievably fit Will Schwalbe and equally fit Ellen Archer. The ever youthful Bob Miller. Ashley "Miss Congeniality" Van Buren. Christine Ragasa. Miriam Wenger. Christine Casaccio. Katie Wainwright. Claire McKean. Cassie Mayer, who first suggested this book. Michelle Ishay, for her incredible cover.

My tireless readers: Pal Irish and Richard Rodriguez, who painstakingly helped me rethink, rough up, slim down, fatten up, and talk some sense into countless drafts. My *New York Observer* editor, Peter Stevenson. My support staff: Amy Witkoff, Rachel Berman, Lulie Haddad, Ellen Biben, Jen Unter, Michelle Nader, Sarah Brysk Bridge, and Sarah Dunn. Patricia "Ian keeps asking me when you're Going to Finish Your Book" Murrell. Joyce McFadden, without whom I might have written every story in crayon in a tattered robe and slippers at a "rest facility." Phyllis Rose, who read my early writing, which was about as intelligible as ink blots, and encouraged me to keep going long after she had to.

Finally, thank you so much to all the witty, smart, engaging people mentioned in the pages of this book. I hope that you know that you're in the book because you're utterly memorable. I owe you so much and thank you for all of it.

It's never too late to be what you might have been.

—George Eliot

· 1 ·

THE FIXER-UPPER

I GREW UP thinking my mother had the answer to everything. Watch any black-and-white film and she always knew some obscure fact about an actor with one line. "See the fishmonger behind the ox, the one who's yelling, 'Slay the hunchback!' " she'd say. "His name was Skids Monroe. He came out of the Yiddish theater and was tragically maimed in a Ferris wheel accident."

She knew about words.

"The term 'steatopygous' means characterized by fat about the hips and buttocks," she explained. She grabbed a pillowy section of her thigh just below her tennis skirt, adding, "All of this, right here, is steatopygia, and once it was considered not cellulite, but a highly desirable benchmark of fertility!" She pointed at me. "Remember that next time you say you look hideous in a bathing suit."

And she knew about men.

For my mother there were only two answers to any question involving love: he'd be back, or I was better off without him.

At sixteen, when my first boyfriend, Cliff Green, said we should see other people, I was crushed, despairing in a way I'd never experienced. "My life is over!" I wept.

"Sweetheart, I know you're upset, but give me the knife," my mother said, when I took to eating whole pound cakes in one sitting.

She began her pep talk, as she often did, by free-associating. "We all liked Cliff, and it's probably time I told you that although you and your father thought it was your little secret, I knew Cliff snuck out of the house every morning. I could hear him tromping through the living room, then slamming the kitchen door."

I was sitting on a low stepladder, my elbows resting on my knees, scraping the cream filling out of a pile of soggy Oreos I planned to put back in the cookie jar. My mother was standing behind me, wearing a flowered navy and yellow kimono we had picked out together on our trip to Japan. Her hair stopped just below her chin. It was entirely gray by this point, a crisp platinum, but her face remained almost without a wrinkle. Her wide, soft cheeks, modest nose, and lively hazel eyes looked much the way they had a decade before.

"I'm glad that you confided in me about being depressed about your relationship. At first I was afraid you and Cliff were smoking pot and that's why you had the munchies," she said, using a new bit of slang she'd learned at the "*Just Say No to Drugs*" sisterhood luncheon at the synagogue. She tossed out an empty quart of butter pecan ice cream I'd eaten and another of mint chip from which I'd systematically picked out all the chips. "But now that I know you're depressed, the long afternoon naps make sense." She stood behind me tenderly picking cookie crumbs out of my hair.

"Pussycat, trust me. I'm positive. He'll be back."

"You really think so?"

"Mark my words," she said. "I promise."

Two months later, Cliff came back.

When I fell in love with a boy named Ian, freshman year of college, who told me he loved me in a way he had never loved anyone before, enough to admit to me and only me that he was gay, his mascara smearing as he wept, my mother consoled me with "Better now than in thirty years." She put her arm around me. "Could you really get serious with a man who wore a bustier?" Adding finally, "You're better off without him."

At twenty-four, Jay McPhee ended our relationship of two years explaining that, while his preferred model of love was "The Dog Bone"—namely two separate, independent entities bound by a long, sturdy bridge (he said "long" twice, as in "long, long sturdy bridge")—my ideal was what he called "The Pretzel," where two people are twisted together, fused in several places, preventing any opportunity for individuality. Or escape.

"I'm not a pretzel," I said, desperately.

"Oh, but you are," he said.

"I can be a dog bone!" I pleaded. "I can! Give me a chance!"

I didn't think Jay and I were right for each other, but I had always hoped it would be my choice, not his, whether to suffer a life of regret and stifling mediocrity.

"He said you weren't independent? That's ridiculous," my mother said, reaching for the overnight bag I'd brought to stay at my parents' apartment until I felt better. She led me into my old bedroom, still decorated with the many cat posters I collected before we found out I was allergic.

"Not independent." She scoffed. "Mark my words. He'll be back." And when that never happened, she assured me, "You're better off without him."

Right around the time I turned twenty-six, when I reluctantly broke up with David Orlean because he complained I was too independent and career minded, my mother added a new saying to her repertoire.

"People who want to be married are married," she said, thrilled to have coined a phrase that could be so deep and yet so simple.

"Huh?" I said. "I don't get it."

"People who want to be married are married," she repeated. "Look at that woman, the one I showed you in the paper, who's blind now because her husband threw acid in her eyes. Even though she knew he had mistresses, even though he maimed her, she stayed married to him."

She nodded and folded her arms, as if to say, "Am I a genius or what?"

I was confused. "Okay. And?"

"So if you really wanted to be married, you would be!" She clapped her hands in a single loud strike. "That's the answer. When you really want it, it will happen."

A YEAR LATER it still hadn't happened and I was really starting to want it. There had been another David. This time it was David Soloway, a man I'd met in Los Angeles, where I'd just graduated from film school. He was dedicated to me and talked often about marriage, but we had problems. He always wanted me to wear short shorts, the kind I thought should only be worn by women who referred to their boss as "my pimp," and he mentioned often that he didn't judge women who got breast jobs. Or liposuction. At any age. He could also be very critical. He once told me about an ex-girlfriend who'd purred in his ear, "I want you inside of me." "I want you inside me?" he said with disgust. "What kind of thing was that to say? Say, 'I need that huge, hard cock in my hot box,' or 'Your cock is so fucking huge just looking at it makes me come,' or just 'Fuck me with that unbelievably huge cock,' but 'I want you inside me'? Was that supposed to turn me on?"

I was sad after we broke up. I knew it was the right thing,

but still I found myself wondering how many chances you get in life to find the right person. Did you get three? Five? Less? Had I already blown it and just didn't know it yet? Should I have held on to him because I might not find anything better? I had also recently weathered the unanimous rejection of the first screenplay I'd ever written. It was called *Pleased to Meet Me,* about a chronically depressed thirty-year-old single woman who hates her life and goes back in time to prevent her teenage self from growing up to be a thirty-year-old single woman who hates her life. My hope was that it would be a feel-good comedy for the Zoloft set, proof that overwhelming psychological issues, immune to both therapy and medication, could be easily reversed with the aid of a time machine. While I got a few studio meetings out of it, in the end there was no sale. I was a big, pacing, jittery loser in work and love, and once again there was my mother, eager to put me back together.

"What you need is a trip to Prague in May with me!" she announced.

In the past the two of us had traveled together to places like China, Japan, and Holland. We went to Beijing and Shanghai in the late seventies, where we sampled jellyfish, sliced webbed duck's feet, and something we were later told was braised snake. When we were in Amsterdam, we rented a car to explore the countryside, and my mother accidentally drove the wrong way down a single bicycle path, where angry riders threw apples at our windshield. "I thought the Dutch were supposed to be so peaceful," my mother said as we scraped applesauce off the front hood.

And now she wanted us to visit Prague, a city she felt promised both exciting architecture and the possibility of more adventures. She told my father he'd have to fend for himself for ten days, and off we went. The flight was easy, and everything was proceeding smoothly until we went through immigration. Everyone else moved promptly through the line, and then they got to us. The official looked confused as he examined my mother's form.

"What this mean?" he said, his heavily lidded eyes narrowing.

I looked at her form. "Mom, did you *have* to write that?"

She smiled when she realized what he was pointing at.

"I'm a career volunteer," she explained. "That's my profession. I raise money for charities that support communities becoming self-sufficient. We build hospitals and schools, but I don't receive a salary."

He shrugged and stamped her passport.

In the cab to the hotel, my mother repeated her delight at the wonderful rate we'd gotten.

"The hotel is right in the heart of the city," she said. "I done good."

That's what we thought until we got to the hotel and found out it was under renovation. My first thought upon seeing our room was that it had been designed by an architect who specialized in third world prisons. The bed seemed like something a monk would sleep on after he'd forsaken his worldly possessions. As if that wasn't bad enough, our window was boarded up with a splintery piece of wood to keep out the dust from the construction site outside. When the bellboy tried to tell us what time breakfast was served, he had to yell over the sound of wrecking balls and heavy machinery. We tried to switch hotels, but it was May, and the only thing available was forty minutes outside the city.

"Okay," my mother said. "So we won't spend any time in the hotel. Who wants to anyway?"

APPARENTLY, WORKERS START very early in Prague. We were up at six. When I looked outside, I saw a bunch of mustached men, smoking and drinking black coffee, listening to fast-paced accordion music.

My mother and I started the day with what I had heard called the "Jewish Quarter," but which the concierge referred to as "Jew Town," which sounded to me like a theme park that would be filled with rides such as "The Emotional Roller Coaster."

"Do you think he was anti-Semitic?" I asked as we left the hotel.

"Oh, you and your paranoia," she said. "No, I don't think he was an anti-Semite. And I don't think the cabdriver was either," she said, referring to our ride from the airport. "I think it was an unfortunate translation when he called us 'Jew People.' "

We proceeded to Josefov, the Jewish Quarter. My mother read the guidebook out loud as we walked.

"The area was named in honor of Emperor Joseph II of the Austrian Empire, which ruled the Czech Republic in the eighteenth century. Emperor Joseph issued the Tolerance Edict in 1781, which revoked the old law that required Jews to wear distinctive caps and Stars of David on their clothing." She put the book back in her bag. "Well, thank God for that. See, this city was very progressive when it came to Jews." She snapped a photo of the Hebrew clock, which had numbers in Hebrew and ran backward. It sat at the top of a mauve building with an elaborate baroque facade. It was early, and the streets were empty as we walked toward the "Old-New" synagogue next door.

That's when I felt a tap on my shoulder. The young man was probably twenty-five and sublimely handsome. He had shoulder-length black hair, blue eyes, and was dressed in an oatmeal V-neck sweater and jeans. He had an ethereal beauty that said, "You can look, but you can't touch." Poets would write about beauty like his. Which made me think of the Shakespeare sonnet "Shall I compare thee to a summer's day?" Then I thought of what Shakespeare might have said about me. "And this one to a humid night in Newark."

"Are you Jewish?" the young man asked.

I clenched my teeth and looked at him. "Why?"

My mother interrupted, placing a hand on each hip. "Yes, we are Jewish. And deeply proud of it."

"Me too," he said, cheerfully. He held out his hand. "My name is Miguel. I am from Argentina."

"Hello, Miguel." My mother held out her hand. "I'm Joyce Arnoff-Cohen." She always used the hyphenate. It was a throwback to her interest in feminism in the early seventies, when, for a short time, she went bra-less and paraded around in a neon maxicoat trimmed in knotty yak fur. "And this is my daughter, Amy Cohen."

Miguel smiled. "Very nice to meet you, Amy and Joyce. May I join you?"

"We'd be delighted," my mother said.

At lunch, we found out Miguel had planned to come with his brother, but he'd gotten into a soccer accident which had resulted in a minor head injury.

"I'm studying to become a pediatrician," Miguel told us.

"Bravo!" my mother said.

"Amy, do you like children?" he asked.

"Not like, *love*," I said, laying on my best earth mother shtick. "I can't wait to have my own."

"Me too," he said, winking. "My mother would like me to have them tomorrow. I think I will be ready soon." He pushed his plate toward me. "Amy, would you like the rest of my salad? It's very nice."

"No, thank you," I said, but what I really wanted to say was "I'll have your children."

A Jewish Argentinean doctor. And as if Miguel weren't perfect enough already, when we went to the Jewish cemetery, he cried. Not sobbed, just a single elegant tear gliding down one of his perfectly molded cheeks. I gave him a napkin I'd taken from the restaurant, and he tapped the corner of his eye.

He took my hand and held it for a moment. "Thank you," he said. "I just have so much feeling being here. All we have endured and fought for. All the people who were lost."

We stood amid the headstones—some fat, some tall, all clustered together. My mother was crying too, but she'd started crying as we entered the front gate.

"Miguel, that's beautiful," she said, blowing her nose.

I was very moved being there myself, and yet all I could think was "How can I get rid of my mother?"

"Miguel, I hope you'll join us for dinner," my mother said.

"Yes," he said. "I was hoping you would ask, Joyce."

Then he kissed us each on both cheeks and said, "Until later."

We watched him walk away, and when we were sure he was out of sight, my mother said, "He's a devastatingly attractive young man. For him, I'll come visit you in Argentina."

"Slow down there, partner," I said, as much to myself as to her.

"Sweetheart, a mother can dream, can't she? I saw him staring at you not once, not twice, but several times today."

"No. Really?"

She folded her arms and nodded. "Yes, really. The only reason I invited him to join us in the first place was for you. Sometimes you need your mother to push things along."

Okay, I thought. I'll ditch her after dinner.

. . .

We chose what we had been told was the best restaurant in Prague. It was actually a large apartment, which had been divided into several intimate, formal dining rooms, each with only a few tables.

When Miguel arrived, he looked even more handsome than I'd remembered. He was wearing a slim, navy wool, single-button suit with a rich blue V-neck sweater underneath. He was so continental, and I was so local. He was the Riviera. I was the East River. This was the early nineties, when granny boots and T-shirts worn under loose apron dresses were big. I had worn this, my favorite outfit, specially for the occasion. I also had on earrings, big hoops. I rarely wore earrings, because I thought they made me look like a gypsy, and true to my fear, I now felt as if I should be banging a tambourine and pick-pocketing tourists in a crowded marketplace.

"You two look very beautiful," he said.

I imagined kissing him. Standing under one of the dramatic arches we'd seen that day, on a cobblestone street in my long apron and granny boots. I'd press that gorgeous Argentinean face into mine. He'd whisper something in my ear like "I couldn't wait for dinner to be over. I couldn't wait to be alone with you." I just had to be careful not to drink too much since I was very nervous.

"Joyce, your necklace is so unusual," Miguel said.

My mother was wearing a thin red sweater and a heavy

silver necklace that my brother, sister, and I thought looked like an enlarged, diseased organ.

"I got this from a sculptor in Tel Aviv," she said. "He usually does large installations using scrap metal from cans. My children hate this necklace, don't you?"

"We call it 'The Liver,'" I said, smiling at Miguel. I kept smiling, then smiled some more, but he didn't look at me. Instead, he stared at my mother.

"Oh, no. It's very artistic," Miguel said. "Besides, calling it 'The Liver' is actually a compliment because of all that the liver does."

"I didn't do so well in biology," I said. "Our biology teacher turned out to be making extra money doing porn and he got fired midyear."

"That's nice." He turned to my mother. "The liver is our filter. It keeps us alive. It's the most important organ in the body," Miguel said, moving so close to my mother that his face was inches from hers. "Next to the heart." He held out his hand. "Joyce, may I touch it?"

"Why, of course," my mother said.

I watched as he lifted the heavy, pear-shaped bulb in the center of her chest. "Fantastic," he said, staring not at the necklace but deep into my mother's eyes, the way I imagined he had looked at me when I offered him the tissue at the cemetery, the brief moment I'd been replaying in my head all day. This was before I began imagining how he would spend his next vacation visiting me in Los Angeles.

I pictured us spending the entire time holed up in my dark, slightly depressing apartment. When we could manage to tear ourselves away from each other, I'd take him to one of those parties that feel so quintessentially L.A., the kind where you're waiting for the keg and realize John Stamos and Dave Grohl are standing behind you. Then, at the end of the evening, I'd wave good-bye to my friends, all successful screenwriters, and think that, despite my being a total failure with a career in the crapper, at least I had a hot Argentinean boyfriend who might one day love me.

When the waiter came, Miguel was still holding on to my mother's necklace as if it were glued to his fingers. "Joyce. It's clear you have a very stylish eye," Miguel said.

The waiter, a thin man with a bold black mustache that carpeted his lip, stood at the table holding two bottles of wine, waiting for my mother to notice him. I kicked my mother's foot under the table, trying to tell her that the waiter had been standing there, but Miguel looked at me and frowned. "That's my foot," he said, releasing her necklace.

"Mom, that one looks good," I said, pointing to the more expensive of the two.

Taking my suggestion, my mother looked up at the waiter. "We'll take that one."

"Excellent choice, Joyce," Miguel said. "Clearly, you know wine."

"I know I like it," my mother said. "But I'd hardly call myself an expert. I've been an expat, when I lived in England after the war, but never an expert."

Miguel laughed. An expansive, rollicking belly laugh. I wasn't even convinced he understood what she'd said. "Joyce, you're very funny," he said. Then he turned to me. "Does everyone tell her how funny she is?"

"Not really," I said. I downed my glass of wine and filled another one.

"Lying will get you everywhere," my mother said. "But Amy's the funny one. Miguel, guess what Amy does. Actually, sweetheart, you tell him. It's very exciting."

"Mom, no, really." I waved my hand back and forth along my throat, pantomiming for her to cut what she was saying.

Miguel kept his eyes fixed on my mother as he reluctantly turned toward me. "What do you do?" he asked.

"I just graduated from film school," I said. "I wrote a screenplay, which didn't get bought. End of story."

I stared at my empty glass, waiting for Miguel to pour me another one, as he was doing for my mother.

"Oh, come on now," my mother said. "It was much more exciting than that. Tell him what the film was about."

"It's about a woman who goes back in time to meet herself as a teenager," I said, as if my words were on a forced death march. "She's very unhappy as an adult, so she tries to prevent herself from growing up to be such an unhappy person. Etc. Etc."

He didn't say anything at first; it seemed as if he were

ruminating about the cleverness of my script. But then he looked not at me, but somewhere off in the distance. "Why have Hollywood movies become so mindless?" he asked. "I don't mean yours," he finally added, which made it absolutely clear that he did. "Are people so desperate for money?"

"Well, it *is* Hollywood," I said, feeling rather desperate myself. I reached across the table for the bottle of wine that was now in front of him. "I just wanted to make people laugh. This was my first script."

"And is that a reason to do it?" he said. "The world needs *The Deer Hunter* and *The Battle of Algiers*. Not another mindless comedy."

Before I could defend myself and mention that I was a huge fan of both of those movies, having seen each several times, Miguel turned to my mother. "Joyce, what do you do?"

She sat up very straight, and I knew what was coming. "I'm a career volunteer," she said. "Which means that—"

"I understand," he interrupted. "You work for a charity. How excellent. Tell me all about that. I'm terribly interested because I was thinking for a time that I wanted to go into the Peace Corps. To devote my life to public service. And my parents approved. My father spent a short time working in Africa with Dr. Schweitzer."

"But they had to settle for a doctor?" my mother said, proud of her joke.

He laughed keenly. "Yes, sad, isn't it? No, no, I thought, and my father agreed, with a medical degree I'd be more help in an

AIDS ward." He smiled perfunctorily at me, as if to say, "See, not everybody is so desperate to make money." Then he turned back to my mother. "I just see so many people doing such self-indulgent things with their lives."

My glass was empty now and so was the bottle. I had no choice but to steal my mother's wine.

"Miguel, when Amy was in high school she raised money for Oxfam," my mother said. "She was always very involved."

Miguel pointed dramatically in her direction. "That's because you're such a wonderful mother. You've impressed upon your children how important it is to think of others." Then he turned to me. "Do you volunteer now? You probably want to get away from yourself sometimes."

This was about the time I finished eating my pork neck in dill sauce and began eating the rest of my mother's goulash.

"Last month I painted Christmas decorations at a home for juvenile delinquents," I said, spearing several cubes of slick meat and shoving them into my mouth. "I painted snowflakes with a kid who robbed a Seven-Eleven."

"Well, that's something," he said. "Joyce, does everyone tell you that you look very young? It's amazing."

"I think you were out in the sun too long," she said. "But that's lovely of you to say."

"Are you two done?" I said.

Miguel looked at me, and I pointed to the waiter standing to my left.

"He wants to take our plates," I said.

"Oh, yes," my mother said.

"Thank you," Miguel added.

"Miguel, I've been so good all day," my mother said. "But I just can't contain myself. Do you have a girlfriend?"

Miguel became very bashful and stared at his lap, and as he did, I mouthed to my mother, "Cut it out." She batted her hand at me, as if to say, "Oh, shush." This reminded me of the time I told my mother I'd met a witty, mildly famous Hollywood producer at a party and immediately developed an insatiable crush on him, and she said, "Call him up and ask him out for a Coke!" Just that feeling of "Mom, what planet are you on?" The Argentinean Jewish doctor didn't like me. Better to forfeit the fight and go home with as little blood as possible.

"Joyce, I'm very available," he said, smiling at her. "Tell me, where is your husband? Are you married?"

"My father had to stay in New York and work," I said. "We called him before we came to dinner. He said he misses us. A lot. He really misses us. He's insanely jealous."

"Well, he's a very lucky man, Joyce," Miguel said. "You have a very special quality. In addition to being very beautiful, you seem like someone I've known a very long time. I imagine you've led a very interesting life."

As my mother told him about her years in postwar England, when she met Anna Freud and ate lentil soup with Alec Guinness, I ate her entire portion of apple strudel and then the generous platter of crepes drizzled in heavy chocolate and cream that was meant to serve three. And then I ordered a plate of fluffy peach dumplings.

"Tomorrow we're going to visit the Kafka sights," my mother said. "I'm salivating. I love Kafka."

Miguel got a dreamy look on his face. "He's my favorite writer," he said. "What are your favorite works?"

I interrupted. "Which is the Kafka story that describes the torturing and killing of prisoners?" I looked at Miguel. "The one that's very brutal with the instrument they called the 'apparatus'?"

" 'In the Penal Colony'!" my mother said, brightly. "Oh, I love that story too. But I still think 'Metamorphosis' is my favorite."

"Me too," Miguel said. "Excellent taste, Joyce."

My mother blushed and then looked over at me. "Oh, sweetheart, you look like you're about to plotz. Let's get you to sleep."

And there it was. There would be no midnight walk. No kissing under any arches, just wrecking balls at six A.M.

As we left the restaurant, Miguel said, "I hope to see you tomorrow," adding clumsily, "both of you."

My mother smiled as she waved good-bye.

"He's in love with you," I said.

"Oh, please. That's ridiculous. That's just the wine talking."

"Yours or mine?" I said. "And I'm not spending the day with him tomorrow."

"Fine. We'll leave the hotel before he calls. Besides, you

know those Latins. They're like Italians. They're all crazy about their mothers, and I'm sure he just wanted me to fill in. It's actually very insulting if you ask me."

THE NEXT MORNING, on our way up to the Prague Castle, we walked along Golden Lane, a row of tiny, colorful cottages built into the castle wall in the sixteenth century to house the castle guard. I was wearing my apron dress again, a painful reminder of our dinner the night before, while my mother was wearing a cheerful plaid blouse, a twill skirt, and coarse, ropy espadrilles that made her heels turn a painful shade of pink.

It was a warm, windless spring day, and we stopped to stand outside of a squat, light blue building where Franz Kafka had lived briefly with his sister.

"I hope you have a kosher wedding," my mother said, reaching deep into her public television tote bag and patting around for her camera. "With Kafka, I just keep wondering what influenced his work. Did he see a cockroach in the kitchen and imagine 'The Metamorphosis'? I know he had TB, and I think he was starving to death when he wrote 'A Hunger Artist.' " She regarded the small building, looking up at the second-story window. "Was he in love when he lived here? Was he depressed?" She smiled. "It's fun to imagine, isn't it?"

I looked at her, not exactly sure how to react.

"What are you talking about?" I said. "My wedding? I don't even have a boyfriend."

"I know," she said, framing a shot of the house, careful to include the heavy shingled roof. "I'm just saying when. When you have your wedding, I hope it's kosher. I wouldn't want my kosher friends to have to eat from paper plates."

Why I chose to argue about this, I still don't know.

"How many kosher friends do you have?" I asked.

She began to count.

"Well, there's Rabbi Hershkowitz and his wife, Tsipora—that's two. And Sam and Audrey Bloom—so four. I'd like to invite the Yarones from Israel, which makes six, but I doubt they'd come."

I've read that nothing travels faster than the speed of light, but I think a close second might be the rate at which I went from age twenty-seven to thirteen.

"No, I don't want a kosher wedding," I said, my arms now tightly crossed. "What if I want to serve shrimp?"

"You don't love shrimp," my mother said. "Why do you need shrimp?"

"Because maybe my guests will want it. Or my fiancé."

"You could have mock shrimp," she said.

"I'm not having mock shrimp. If we're having mock shrimp, we might as well have mock ham. Or why don't we just have a mock wedding?"

"You really feel that strongly?" she said.

"I'm thinking very seriously of eloping."

"Why not make it completely vegetarian?" she said, a reference to the ten years I'd gone without meat. "When I took that class on the history of Judaism, we learned that the basis of kashrut is, in fact, vegetarianism, which seems right up your alley. We could have an Indian theme with curries and papadams. There are still Jews in India."

"I—" I started to say something, but instead exhaled, thickly.

"You what?" she said. "You what? Tell me, sweetheart."

"I don't want to have this conversation," I said. "This is crazy."

"Well, I hope you change your mind," she said.

I could tell she was upset by the hasty way she began marching up the hill.

"Are you coming?" she called.

I didn't answer.

She started back. "I asked if you were coming." She got closer to me. "Sweetheart, are you crying?"

I couldn't quite catch my breath, and when I finally spoke, I took long gasps every few words.

"I just feel like men don't like me. Or they like me for a little while and then I screw it up."

"What are you talking about? Everyone loves you."

"No, they don't. Mom. They don't. Not even close."

"Oh, rubbish. Yes, they do."

"I didn't tell you, but before I left, I started seeing this really cute screenwriter who I'd had a crush on for a long time and who just broke up with his girlfriend, and I'm such an idiot, because he just broke up with her, and it was a recipe for masochism, but we fooled around a lot, we didn't sleep together but"—I stopped long enough to catch my breath—"but we saw each other a lot and then I offered to make him dinner. That fettucine recipe that I made you—"

"Which I loved," she said. "It's your best dish."

That was so my mother. To say it was my best dish, when I only had one. "And I spent over fifty dollars. And I also baked him a Duncan Hines cake, like an idiot, and—"

My mother put her arm around me. "And he broke up with you."

"No! Worse. He never showed up. I called him like five times that night and left these pathetic messages, like 'Oh, hey, did you forget?' Like a fucking loser. If I had any self-respect, I would have called and said, 'Fuck you! You lying piece of shit! Go to hell!' But I didn't. Instead I ate the entire cake, and then he didn't call me back for over a week. When he did finally call, he said he'd forgotten about dinner and that he had gone to Wisconsin for a week, and I knew he was lying, and I didn't even let him have it then. I said, 'That's okay, I understand,' because I'm a sheep. I just felt like such a stupid, stupid piece of stupid shit because I should have known. Which is how I feel a lot these days, Mom. Like shit. I do."

She was silent.

I had often said I felt like a house men were happy to rent, but when it came time to buy, they balked. Several boyfriends had told me that being in a relationship with me required work. A lot of extensive work. I was not the brand-new house with central air and freshly polished hardwood floors, the one that was ready to move into immediately. I was the fixer-upper with plenty of room for improvement, one the real estate agent says "could be a gem if you're willing to do an enormous, exhausting amount of work." I was the house in desperate need of renovation. And if I kept eating the way I was on this trip, I'd be the biggest house on the block.

"Let me tell you something," my mother said. "You are the furthest thing from shit. You are beautiful and wonderful and so creative, and by the way, that's my daughter you're talking about and I might have to punch you in the nose if you say you're shit again."

"Mom, I'm serious."

"After I got divorced, I got knocked around myself all the time before I met your father," she said.

My mother had married a psychiatrist at twenty-one, who, she said, loved baseball, Freud, Groucho Marx, and her—in that order.

"I was a divorcée in the days when it was still considered shocking, and I think maybe that's why I had low self-esteem and chose such terrible men. I went out with an alcoholic who worked for the Associated Press, when he wasn't having blackouts and canceling dates with me, and then that Broadway producer I told you about, the one who knew Esther Williams and Jimmy Durante, who I know was scheduling our dinners between hopping into bed with showgirls. I got dumped all the time. Constantly. And then I met your father. And he was sweet and honest, and I was ready for a good man because I'd had such first-class shits before him. I married the wrong man the first time, and I almost made the same mistake again, until I realized what was really important to me. And it was all very roundabout the way it happened. Do you get my drift?"

"Uh huh," I said, wiping my nose.

"If you want to know the truth," she said, "I wasn't so impressed with our friend Miguel. He was a little unctuous, if you ask me. Kissing my hand good night? I was half expecting him to click his heels. It was too much. You need someone more original. And I, for one, am really looking forward to meeting him."

"Yeah, well, you and me both," I said.

BUT THAT WOULD never happen. When I was thirty, we found out my mother had an inoperable brain tumor and that she'd be lucky to live a year. She ended up living nineteen months. We were told that her brain would deteriorate rapidly, that each week she'd lose a little more—the ability to spell or even to recognize people she knew well. She accepted that anything she wanted to tell me would have to be soon. So she attempted to put our house in order before she was gone.

"I want you to know that I want Daddy to meet someone," she said. "I do. I want that very, very much and I want you to welcome her."

"Mom, I can't—" I couldn't even finish my sentence.

We were sitting in the den of my parents' apartment. The room was painted in a deep scarlet with two chubby, blue floral sofas stacked with needlepoint pillows. In the corner stood a sculpture my mother loved, an interactive piece where you placed your face in a plastic mask and saw your creepy reflection multiplied. "It's a conversation piece," she announced when she brought it home. "It's like confronting your multiple personalities. I think it's fun."

My mother was in a wheelchair now, a heavy afghan thrown over her legs. She was paralyzed on one side, the result of her recent stroke, the left side of her face drifting toward her chin.

"Please, sweetheart, I know you can do it," she said. "Treat her as a member of the family. Do that for me."

She knew that I'd have trouble welcoming someone new, that I'd resent whoever it was out of loyalty to her. Even with her mind disintegrating, my mother understood this, and even now, she was playing the matchmaker for my father, arranging a relationship with someone we had yet to meet.

"This whole thing," I said, shaking my head. I often spoke in partial sentences in those days, and I was always up for a fight, arguing with people, even when we were on the same side. I had been so angry since my mother was diagnosed. My skin was breaking out. I only wanted to listen to music where people screamed. I fantasized about slamming my fist on the hood of a taxi that swerved too close to me. Or calling up and bawling out all the people who had ever crossed me, including that screenwriter who stood me up for dinner. Anything to unleash my rage.

I looked over at a framed photo of my older brother and sister, Tom and Holly, and me on vacation in Miami in the early seventies, wearing coordinating white outfits and smiling wildly, buzzed from eating the olives out of my father's martini. I remember that was the same vacation when I ate all the soaked fruit out of a pitcher of sangria and then, with my mother chasing after me, ran around the parking lot yelling, "I can fly!" Years later, my mother told me she wished she'd had a net that night, as it took twenty minutes to get me into the car.

"This whole thing sucks," my mother said. "But I'm so lucky, sweetheart. I've had such a good life. And you need to go on and have a happy life because that's the best thing you could do for me. You being so angry is a waste. Right?"

I shrugged.

"I don't know," I said.

"It is," she said. "I'm not angry."

"I know. That's why I'm angry for you."

"But I don't want that," she said. "I told you what I want. Did you hear me?"

I nodded reluctantly.

And it just seemed so right that one of the last things my mother ever did, one of her last wishes, when it felt as if my sorrow and anger might swallow me whole, was to put me back together yet again.

· 2 ·

LOSING FACE

I DIDN'T KNOW the rash on my face was so bad until I went to drop off my dry cleaning. "Oh God! What that on your face?" Sunhee, the woman behind the counter, asked, moving closer to get a better view. "You burn in grease fire?"

"I don't know. I woke up with it this morning," I said. I put a white blouse on the counter and pointed to a ring of polka dots. "That's all salad dressing."

Sunhee put so many stick-on arrows next to each stain, it looked like a painting of Saint Sebastian. As she continued, I examined my face in the mirrored wall behind the cash register, wondering if you could develop a port-wine stain at any age. I touched my cheeks, which felt hot and swollen under my fingertips.

"What the hell?" I mumbled.

I thought about what I'd eaten, what I'd touched, wondering what might produce a reaction this dramatic. Even bad shrimp wouldn't make me look as if I had diaper rash on my face. And as far as I knew I hadn't washed with battery acid. No, it would take something much bigger than either of those things to make me look like this. It would take something like suddenly getting fired from my television writing job of three years, and then, soon after, getting dumped by Josh, the boyfriend I'd hoped to marry, the one I'd imagined growing old with.

That would do it.

"Look painful," Sunhee said, studying me more closely. "You go through windshield of car?"

I couldn't remember when Sunhee started liking me. I think she warmed to me after I thanked her for doing such a good job getting the black bean sauce out of my duvet cover. The next time I came in she asked me excitedly, "You! Guess how old I am!" I examined her wide, flat face; her eyes, obscured by an inch of sea foam eye shadow; her pageboy wedge of thick, black hair.

"Are you forty?" I lied.

"Fifty-two!" she yelled. "Put laundry bag on scale! I fifty-two! I look young, right?"

"So young!" I said.

"Hard to believe I have sixteen-year-old son in military school, right?"

"You must have been a child bride," I said. I thought maybe I'd laid it on too thick until I noticed she was blushing. She remembered me after that; never my name, though. "I know you," she would say. "555-4575. 210 West 71st. No crease. Leave cleaning with doorman."

Sunhee studied my face. In only a few minutes, the welts had turned a deeper shade of purple; they were now the color of a full-bodied Cabernet.

"You get cheap chemical peel?" she asked. "Because I get cheap chemical peel look exactly like that. People ask me if I am burn in fire. I do it when I still live in Korea. I think, 'Okay, my skin looking old. I need chemical peel.' But I don't want spend money, you understand? I want do it cheaper, so I go to woman who do it in her kitchen. I lie on floor. After that everyone think I am in bad fire or factory accident." She pointed to me. "It look exactly like that."

"So how long did it take to get better?" I asked, growing increasingly alarmed.

"Oh, like, um . . ." It seemed she was totaling the amount of time it took her to heal, down to weeks. "Like five years," she said.

I was a little worried, but I figured I'd get some cream or some pills, and whatever was on my face would be gone within a week. And this shows the kind of luck I have. The one time I was actually calm, I had reason to panic. I'd made an appointment with my dermatologist, Dr. Navasky, as he had always been able to cure anything.

"I bet it's nothing," my sister, Holly, assured me. "When Mom was sick, you always said your skin was so horrible."

"And it was," I said, referring to the adult acne that appeared on my face just after my mother was diagnosed and continued to get worse after she died a year ago. "I had welts everywhere. It looked as if someone stomped all over my face in cleats."

"Well," she conceded, "it wasn't great."

I had a long history of psychosomatic ailments, the worst being the eye sties I developed every summer when I went to camp. When I was nine, when my mother had just recovered from her second bout of breast cancer and I was having insomnia and was so attached to her I practically sprouted from her hip, she somehow got the idea it would be good for me to go to sleepaway camp. It actually wasn't a bad idea on its own, but I begged her not to make me go, weeping, as only a nine-year-old can. "Please don't send me away! I can stay here and be a waitress!" She insisted. The day before I was leaving I woke up with my left eye sealed shut and what looked like a peach pit under my eyelid. And so the first day of camp, the day you make the vital first impression which will carry you through the next two months of forced swims and godforsaken nature walks, I got on the bus with enormous, dark glasses with my mother's initials, J.A.C., imprinted in gold script in the lower right-hand corner. A Labrador strapped to a harness would have completed the picture. I was seated next to a plump girl from Lebanon who spoke no English and whose name was Fatima, but whom the counselor mistakenly called "Fat Ma."

When she went home the following week I was left with my only friend, a chubby, freckled girl named Jodie, with whom I bonded, as she had only one eye.

IN THE FIRST weeks after my breakup, I holed up in my apartment, afraid to go out. I would be fine one minute, and then the next, weeping so violently it seemed as if at any moment my head might explode like a cheap Mexican firecracker. I became emotionally incontinent. I wept at my nephew's Gymboree party; during a paraffin manicure with my hands encased in wax mitts; getting my mail. I couldn't sleep. I had panic attacks where I felt as if my heart were pole-vaulting out of my chest. I lost ten pounds because the only thing I could eat was dry cornflakes. I would lie in bed for hours wondering if and when I would ever feel better. Would it be a month? Next fall? Next year? Everyone kept asking when I'd be ready to meet someone. Could they fix me up? And then, very slowly, things began to get the tiniest bit better, with a lot of help from Xanax and a very patient therapist. I told myself this was going to be the summer I returned to the world, and I think because I'd been so afraid I'd never enjoy life again, I was even more excited about it.

I announced to anyone who cared that after two months I thought I was ready to date again, and perhaps because people felt so sorry for me they produced, which was how Andy Gluskin got my number. He called just a few hours after I got home from the dry cleaner.

When he began the conversation by saying, "I feel like blind dates are something out of *Fiddler on the Roof,* but Mitchell said he'd kill me if I didn't call you," I will admit, I had some reservations. Andy's voice was high-pitched and nasal, the kind of voice a sheep might have if it were to say, "I got divorced last year—sometimes I tell people she's dead."

"Okay then," I said.

Later he told me, "When I first got out of Dartmouth, I thought about being an art dealer, but then I thought, 'Can I deal with neurotic, freak artists all day? No way. I don't have the patience for that,' so I became a doctor." He directed the conversation with the precision of a seasoned crossing guard, waving certain topics through and abruptly halting others. He started by saying, "Tell me about working in television," which was halted with "You know what? Let's save that conversation for dinner," while "What do you like to do besides read?" was followed with "Don't you like snowboarding or golf?"

Sometime during his description of the summer he spent in Alaska canning salmon, I started to look forward not only to meeting him, but to dating in general. At thirty-three, I'd been worried about reentering the dating scene as a single woman in her thirties, a population I was assured was exploding faster than the Chinese birthrate before the government implemented the one-child rule. Because it had been such a long time, I had forgotten that dating was actually very simple and often involved little more than listening to someone like Andy Gluskin describe getting the salmon smell out of his flannel shirt and trying to pick up plump Eskimo women at bars. We made dinner plans for Friday night. Finally, I was getting my life back.

That night, I tried on various outfits I thought I might wear. There was the "Trying Too Hard to Seem Artsy" outfit, which involved a swingy green suede coat I'd gotten at a flea market in Barcelona. It was a coat that said, "I have the heart of a painter even though I don't actually paint." There were safe outfits—monotonous jeans paired with listless T-shirts. There was the "Since it's our first date I'll try to look feminine and pretty, even though I never dress like this, so don't get used to it" outfit. This one involved a glossy fuchsia skirt that might have been fine, if the startling shade of pink had not so perfectly matched the color of the welts on my face. Now I couldn't wait to get to Dr. Navasky's office, if only so I wouldn't have to answer questions from my doorman like "Jesus. Amy. You got the measles?"

Dr. Navasky's office was just what you might expect from someone who believed sound medicine and glitz should never mix. I had tried more glamorous dermatologists, doctors who created their own cosmetic lines and who claimed to have treated Naomi Campbell and Kathie Lee Gifford, but I always returned to Dr. Navasky. His waiting room looked like a hastily organized yard sale: piles of magazines stacked on a card table; a painting of fruit that looked as if it came from an art show held at an airport hotel; an old, battered black leather and chrome sofa, something an aging Italian bachelor might keep to remember his decadent youth. As I waited on the couch, I sat across from a woman who chatted in Yiddish on her cell phone while constantly scratching her cinnamon-colored wig. She looked at me, making a face as if she were smelling something awful. I knew this look, as I'd been guilty of it myself a few times. It was the look that said, "If he's such a good doctor, why do you look like that?"

"Long time no see!" Dr. Navasky said as he entered the tiny examining room. "Are you married? Do you have any kids?"

"Not yet," I said. "And if you don't help me, I don't think I'm going to have either anytime soon."

Dr. Navasky was tall and broad, with a wavy slick of dyed black hair he parted below his left ear and combed all the way past his right. He put his hands on his hips and stared at me.

"Eesh. What did you do to yourself, kiddo?"

He moved closer to contemplate my face, wearing a light on his head and these crazy, thick magnifying glasses, the kind usually seen on chess prodigies. I remember feeling very anxious when he finally pulled off his rubber gloves and threw them in a small plastic pail, as it reminded me of what surgeons do on television when they announce, grimly, to the rest of the operating staff, "Don't blame yourselves. We did everything we could to save her."

Dr. Navasky exhaled deeply, looking at the floor. Then he sat on a tiny, round stool and rolled over to me.

"I'm worried," I said.

"I think this current rash was probably connected to the stress-induced acne you developed when your mother was sick," he said. "But there's also the possibility this is an allergy, and if it is, it's only going to get worse."

"Worse?" I hadn't considered worse. "Will I have to join a leper colony?"

He took a deep breath. "In order to rule out the possibility of allergies, you can only eat steamed vegetables plain, no salt, no pepper, for at least a month. After that, if you get better, we can try adding brown rice, and then, maybe a month later, steamed chicken, but that's iffy. Plus, I don't want you to leave your apartment unless it's absolutely necessary. They said this is going to be a very humid July. Both the heat and the cold can make your skin worse, and you need to be someplace cool—not cold—and very, very dry. Got that?"

I shook my head. "No. I have a first date tomorrow night. We're going out to dinner, and now I can't eat anything and—" I realized I'd forgotten to ask the most important question. "This is going to get better, right? Aren't there any pills you can give me?"

"I think I know what this is," he said. "And if I'm right"—he put his hand on my shoulder—"even with pills, it's going to get worse—much, much worse—before it gets better."

This was the kind of experience you heard described by people on an *Oprah* episode called "My Descent into Hell," or even "Medical Nightmares." You felt sorry for them, but relieved that it wasn't you.

"How long are we talking about?" I asked.

"Anywhere from three months to a year," he said. "If you're lucky."

I didn't cry. First of all, it hurt to cry, as the salt stung my skin. Looking back now, I don't think it had really hit me yet. I just couldn't believe that one more bad thing had happened. My father, who hadn't seen my face at this point, asked only one thing: "Do not cancel your date. Please, sweetheart, for me."

"I'm not meeting anyone looking like this," I said.

"Don't be silly," my father said. "This young man's a doctor. You think he hasn't seen worse? He probably worked in the emergency room at some point. I bet he's seen people who were shot or in car accidents."

From his peppy delivery, I gathered this was supposed to make me feel better.

"Please, sweetheart, it's so important. You need to get on with your life. You've had such a hard time. You've been so down for so long. You need to move forward and you gotta do this. Please."

His voice was so full of emotion. He'd lost his wife and then a year later watched as his youngest daughter nearly lost her shit. He'd sat with me in diners, in movie theaters, in his living room, as I asked why all this was happening. He drove me out to our house in the Hamptons, hoping to make me feel better, but I just stared out the window, unable to make even simple conversation.

At the time, I felt as if I were one crying jag away from committing myself to a "rest facility," where I would spend my days pacing the ward in my bathrobe and slippers.

I remember when we finally got to the house, my father dropped his bags quickly.

"Sweetheart, I gotta run to the john. I've had to go for the last hour. I wanted to seal my knees shut in the car. I'll be right back, okay, sweetheart?"

I nodded wearily, and then he just stood there.

"What?" I said. "I thought you were going to the bathroom."

He shrugged.

"I'm going to hold it in," he said. "I don't want to leave you like this."

And so now I couldn't tell him no.

When the day of our date arrived, Andy Gluskin called to tell me to meet him at Cafe Luxembourg, a stylish bistro on the Upper West Side. Usually on blind dates you say, "I'll be wearing a blue sweater" or "I'll be the one trying not to look as if I'm searching for my blind date," but this time I had a surefire way for him to spot me.

"Just so you know, I have this weird rash on my face," I said.

"Oh, please. It can't be that bad," he said.

"Oh, it can."

"When I got back from Belize, I had this freakish jungle fungus on my leg and it turned out a bug had burrowed under my shin. And it can't be worse than that."

He was wrong.

"Wow," he said when I met him at the restaurant. "You said it was bad, but what is that?"

He was attractive, with a tan face, which was about one-third nose. His build was small and sturdy. He nervously twisted a tight, blond curl around his finger.

"See, I wasn't kidding," I said.

"Okay," he said, as if bracing himself for combat. "Let's do this."

On certain nights in Manhattan you can feel that in all the world, you are in the epicenter of beauty. In the corner was the six-foot blonde who used to sell lemons in Leningrad, before she was discovered by a modeling agent. The Michelangelo sculpture eating the steak frites at the bar was spotted in a pub in Dingle. The restaurant was packed with genetic wonders, and I looked as if I'd fallen asleep on a George Foreman Grill. We walked the length of the restaurant, past Liam Neeson, on whom I had a tremendous crush, to the banquette against the back wall.

"That looks like it hurts," Andy said, pointing to me. He picked up the wine list. "Red or white?"

"Mmm, actually I'm on this special diet, and I can only have steamed vegetables and water."

"Am I surprised?" he said.

The waiter came by. He had a sweet, effervescent smile, and I knew immediately he did musical theater, because it was the kind of smile you see only in the chorus of *Oklahoma!* or *South Pacific,* doing high kicks and belting it out to the nosebleed seats.

"Are you interested in a glass of wine?" he asked.

Andy looked at me and then at the waiter.

"I'll take a bottle of the Pinot Noir," he said.

He tore off a slice of thick, white bread. We didn't say anything for a few minutes until he said, "You know, Darwin had really bad skin."

Darwin? I wanted to hear that Audrey Hepburn had really bad skin. Or Gwyneth Paltrow. But Darwin?

"Some scientists believe his skin condition was caused by depression. Others think it was lactose intolerance. I was actually part of a study about how the mind can affect the heart."

"And?" I said, fascinated.

"Nothing you don't know. A diseased body can stem from a diseased mind, yadda, yadda, yadda. Like, for example, when I was getting divorced, my ex-wife was rushed to the emergency room." He rolled his eyes. "She called me because she thought she was having a heart attack."

"And was she?"

"I could give a shit. I told her to call her shrink," he said, pouring his second glass of wine. "Not that it helped."

The waiter returned to take our order. He looked at me with such compassion, and this was the first time I realized that this rash was like being a human X-ray, as if people could see right through me. There was no hiding my pain. It was all right there. I could smile, but I couldn't pretend that everything was well and good.

"I can only have steamed vegetables," I explained. "With

no oil or butter or salt. And"—I rolled my eyes—"I need a pan that never had any garlic in it because I might be allergic."

"Fine," the waiter said. "Not a problem."

"Whoa, don't overdo it," Andy said when my steamed vegetables came. "Easy does it on the carrots."

As he poured his fifth glass of wine, I noticed Andy was gazing at a woman at the next table.

"Do you know her?" I asked. It just came flying out. I thought maybe it was someone he knew through his ex-wife. If I'd taken a few more seconds, I would have realized what a stupid question it was.

"Um." He stared at his lap for what seemed like forever, until he looked up at me, making a face that was either embarrassed or apologetic, I couldn't tell which. Then he raised his finger for the check and said, "I'm done."

Afterward I called my friend Eve to tell her what had happened. "And . . . then . . . he kept staring at her and I felt so hideous."

"I'd like to find this guy and cut his fucking balls off," she said. "You know I get very mafioso when it comes to you. I want this guy dead."

"And the worst part is," I said, "now I miss Josh even more."

"Ame, please, let's not idolize Josh. I mean, he was fine and occasionally funny, but average-looking workaholics are a dime a dozen in this town. Plus, let's not forget, every time I called you at his apartment, you could never talk, or you could only talk from his bathroom because he was trying to sleep or he was working and you needed to be quiet. Remember, I used to call you 'Prisoner X432897.' I mean, it was like you were in the Gulag! God forbid the man loses ten minutes of sleep! And have you forgotten the night you got fired? How indifferent he was and then making you call your agent from the bathroom to discuss the rest of your life? I mean, that's not a good situation."

"Right. Remind me of all that," I said. "A lot."

"You should think of yourself as one of those people who walks out of a head-on collision without a scratch. Someone who's lucky to have her life back. Am I making any sense?"

I thought this was an interesting example, given the fact that so many people had told me recently I looked like I'd been in a car accident. "Of course," I said, but just thinking about Josh now made me miss him terribly. I missed little things: the way he dressed like one of the Beastie Boys and that his friends called him "Fresh kid Yid." I loved that once, when I accused him of being passive-aggressive during an argument, he said, "I'm not being passive-aggressive. Just aggressive." I think because I was in so much pain when I met Josh, even the littlest bit of happiness seemed absolutely narcotic. In my head, our story had a happy ending. I fell in love at the worst point in my life. He met my dying mother. We lived happily ever after.

Eve was laughing. "I mean, between me, your father, and your sister, I'm surprised Josh is still walking the streets with his kneecaps in one piece!"

"More, please," I said. "This is all helping."

"I mean, the pathology of these men is so enraging," she said. "You know I'm convinced that half the men in New York have God complexes. And the doctors? Don't get me started. That Andy Toughskin or whatever his name was. He was a doctor, right?"

"Gluskin," I said. "Yes."

"Toughskin, Gluskin, Newskin, Foreskin, who cares? What a loser. Doctors are the worst because they actually believe they *are* God. And these men are never a loving God, who's kind and gentle and helps the meek inherit the earth. These men are always a vicious, punitive God who unleashes floods and wars and plagues because he couldn't get a date in high school."

Hearing her talk about God made me question, yet again, why all these things were happening to me. Not in a "poor me" sort of way, but I began wondering if God was trying to tell me something, and if so, what? I was struggling not only with all the things that had actually happened, but with the idea that I was now the kind of person these things happened to. When I met Josh, everyone told me we were destined to be together: Something bad happens (my mother being so sick) and something wonderful comes along because you deserve it. Josh was that wonderful thing, they all said. That made sense, as it seemed to obey the law of averages, which says that eventually everything evens out. All my life I had found comfort in the law of averages. It never occurred to me that if your mother died, you could lose your job, lose your boyfriend, and then lose your face all within a year's time.

. . .

IN AUGUST, THE humidity made the air thick and gummy. True to Dr. Navasky's prediction, the moisture caused my skin to swell and plump and hurt even more.

My father came over to visit.

"I came to offer you moral support," he said, handing me a bouquet of apricot-colored tulips. "But now I'm thinking maybe I should have brought you some birds. It's like you're living in Alcatraz."

"I can't go out. It's not getting any better," I said.

He examined my face.

"Sweetheart, it's getting better. You can barely see it," he said, as if he were reading off a cue card. Then he looked closer. "Just go to very, very dark places for dinner. And if there's a candle on the table, blow it out. Wait a minute, you know what'll help? I have a terrific idea. I don't know why I didn't suggest this sooner. Maybe put a little makeup on it!"

"I have makeup on it."

"Oh, you do?" he said, wincing. "Really? And Navasky told you if you go outside it could get worse?"

"He said 'much worse.' "

"Well," he said, "at least you have cable."

And so I stayed inside. My apartment building was, at one time, a single-room occupancy hotel, which had been converted into small, one-bedroom apartments, which possessed all the charm of a halfway house. The eggshell paint was peeling. The rooms were dark and noisy, since the building was filled with musicians who spent all day practicing scales. This was the place where I now spent my days, nights, afternoons, mornings, and weekends, in exile, alone. I was Napoleon on Elba. Gordo, the American squirrel monkey, launched into space. I worried I'd become like Tom Hanks having long conversations with a volleyball in *Castaway*. All I did every day was think. I couldn't stop thinking, no matter how hard I tried. My mind was always swimming.

When my mother first got sick, I remember feeling lucky to have such a demanding job that consumed me. For three seasons, I'd written for a show that took place in the New York City mayor's office. Most days we got into work at ten to write and then rewrite, tinker with, add to or subtract from, punch up, cut down, or, if the network had any big notes, completely change the week's script. Our first year, the staff consisted of three women and six men, one of whom had been voted the funniest man in Wisconsin. I'd heard someone say once that writing for a weekly sitcom was like "having your thesis due every week." And I tended to agree. We pitched jokes, story ideas, better endings, better jokes, new stories if a particular character hadn't gotten enough lines that week. We'd work until four in the morning and sometimes even past sunrise, and to keep awake, we'd eat. And eat. The table in the writer's room was always cluttered with food: Wonder bread, Ritz crackers, slices of turkey that were curling around the edges, Skippy peanut butter, American cheese, Doritos, Ruffles, Snickers.

Häagen-Dazs. Oreos. A chocolate chip muffin with the chocolate chips picked out. Diet Coke, Coke, coffee, Snapple. And in the center, an enormous bottle of Rolaids. During some of our more exhausting weeks, I described writing for a sitcom as a "dysfunctional family Thanksgiving," where a group of people are crammed around a table, yelling over one another while eating to the point of discomfort. But more often I loved it and felt lucky because being so busy allowed me to avoid asking questions about my life or myself.

But now, confined to my apartment, I couldn't get away from anything, even from my own worst enemy—me. I watched movies like *The Hunchback of Notre Dame* and *The Elephant Man,* relating deeply to the characters, both of whom died at the end, a fact I couldn't help but notice.

When Eve would call, as she did several times a day, and ask what I was doing, I almost always said, "Lying on my bed. Thinking."

"Thinking or stewing?" she said.

"Thinking, stewing, obsessing, regretting. I like to shake it up."

Every day, I ordered my one meal of steamed vegetables from the same Chinese restaurant, Happy Cottage, where they now knew me. "No garlic in pan, no oil, hello again," the woman said. In addition, constantly worried that I was having a drug interaction that was making my skin worse, I became notorious at my local Rite Aid. "Didn't you call ten minutes ago?" the pharmacist said. "You're the girl with the rash, right?"

The only saving grace in this whole situation was that I'd

saved enough money to live comfortably for a year, so I didn't have to go into an office and confront people and fluorescent lights.

But I missed my job terribly. I loved the show I'd worked on. Even more than that, I loved being a TV writer. Part of the reason why being a TV writer meant so much to me, why it was much more than just a job, had to do with my deep fear that I'd never amount to anything. After college, my first job was teaching English as a second language to newly arrived immigrants, mostly from Russia. Burly Boris Yeltsin types would greet me in the morning by saying, "Emmy, you know what is good idea? Good idea, tomorrow you wear very short skirt and see-through top. We think is good idea!" Next, I was an assistant to a moody magazine editor who, though a severe diabetic, enjoyed furtive lunches of sugary pound cake and gin. The editor had a terrible stammer, and I was an even more terrible assistant. Every morning, I would cower in my cubicle, waiting for him to yell, "Ay!" At which point I would head into his office only to hear, "Mee! How can you be so stooo!" His face grew redder as he waved something I'd misfiled or typed wrong. "So stoo! So stoo!" he repeated, until he let out a final "Pid!" Ultimately, I spent so much time in the bathroom hiding from this man, people could only assume I either had a coke problem or bulimia. So for me, being a TV writer afforded a certain level of validation. Everyone thought I was this huge idiot, and now I made money from it.

In the first weeks after I was fired, my father had all sorts of ideas about what I could do. "What about working with the elderly or with retarded children?" he said. "You have such a nice way with people, and you could get a social work degree."

"But I don't have any interest in social work," I said.

"But that's now. Sy Sussman's daughter, Debbie, works with people with cerebral palsy, and she just loves it! She's so happy. Maybe that's something you should consider."

I knew I lacked the dedication necessary for social work, which left the question: what was I going to do with my life? Who was I going to be now? I could go back to television, but there were so few TV jobs in New York I'd probably have to move to Los Angeles. I could design handbags. Or write a book. Or go to South Africa and work with AIDS orphans for a few months. Or get a teaching degree in something.

"MAYBE YOU GOT this rash so you wouldn't have to decide what to do," my sister, Holly, said, during her daily morning phone call.

"Okay, could everyone please stop playing Freud?" I said.

I was referring to the new parlor game everyone seemed to be playing: Why did Amy get this rash?

My therapist suggested that perhaps the rash was a way of protecting myself. "If no one can get close to you," she said, "you can't get hurt." She compared it to when I gained a great deal of weight in high school. "That was a way of protecting yourself also."

"From what?" I said. "My old jeans?"

My friend Ray asked why I thought I carried my stress in my face. "I mean, you could have thrown your back out or gotten another eye sty, but no. It's on your face. Why? Think of the metaphors."

"The metaphors? Who are you, Susan Sontag?"

"Think about it." I could hear his voice getting more animated, and I could tell he was loving this. "Losing face, being ashamed, which you were when Josh dumped you and you got fired. Facing facts, which you now have to do. Recently your life went from pretty good to shitty—an about-face. It's all there."

"Facing myself," I said.

"Yeah. Maybe this is all about facing yourself."

"Oh God. Now I have to face myself too?"

It occurred to me that perhaps the reason I was so annoyed with everyone was because I knew there was an element of truth in what they were saying. Now their parlor game became mine. What was this rash, and why had I gotten it? Maybe I still had a lot to talk about. My feelings about my mother dying. My feelings about being fired. My feelings about being ditched by a man who only a week before had told my family he was planning to marry me. It was at my cousin's wedding and we were taking photos and my aunt said, playfully, "Only family members in the photos" and Josh said, "Well, I'm going to marry Amy." At which point my father said "Mazel tov!" throwing his hands over his head like a referee confirming a touchdown. The rest of my family—my sister, her husband, and their two kids, and my brother, his wife, and their two kids, said they'd assumed the announcement was coming any day. There were hugs and handshakes. Josh and I danced to a klezmer version of "Kung Fu Fighting" as I pictured the first dance at our own wedding. Seven days later he ended things, saying, "I just can't do it. It's too much pressure and I'm freaking out." I was in so much pain when all that happened, just excruciating, rambling pain. I thought I'd gotten to the other side, but maybe I hadn't.

I remembered a conversation I'd had with my sister right after I moved out all of the stuff I kept at Josh's apartment. I was telling her how I felt as if everything in my life was so abstract now, that I had no concrete way of describing myself. And she said, "That's not true. Your family loves you and you're terrific!"

And I snapped, "Imagine if you had no children and no husband and no job. How would you describe yourself then? How would you even think of yourself?"

And she said, "I don't know."

Is it worse to lose everything you have or to never have anything at all? I think people so often assume it's worse to lose something—a boyfriend, a job, a parent. And yes, those losses are horrible; I knew that as well as anyone could. But I can also say that not having things—looking out into your future and seeing only an amorphous idea of what's to come—is scary too, because no matter how active you are in trying to get the things you want, you feel vulnerable to the emptiness that's waiting to be filled.

. . .

T. S. ELIOT CALLED April the "cruelest month," but for me it was a tie between September and October. Now I understood what Dr. Navasky meant by much worse. Every morning I had no idea what I'd find. One day I'd wake up and my eyes would have mushroomed during the night, like at the end of *Rocky* when his eyes are so engorged he's yelling, "Cut me, Mick. Cut me!" Or I would be so puffy my face looked like a purple down jacket.

I began going to Dr. Navasky's office to get cortisone shots. After a few weeks, his nurse said, "Amy, why don't I put you in Dr. Navasky's personal office. You can read *Vogue* magazines in there and make phone calls if you want. It's much nicer." I knew she was just trying to find a kind way to tell me they didn't want me to wait with the other patients. The week before, there had been an incident. I was waiting with two heavyset Hasidic men both wearing long coats in the middle of a prolonged Indian summer. When I came in, the two men were having a conversation.

"Shmulik, why are you standing up?" the bigger of the two said. "It's making me nervous. You're like one of those guards at Buckingham Palace, just standing there. Sit! Please."

"I have sciatica in my hip," Shmulik said. "It feels better to stand. That upsets you?"

When I shut the door, they both turned and looked at me.

After they'd been talking so much, now we all sat in silence, until Shmulik finally asked, "Miss, is that contagious?"

So now, even when I tried to be with other people, I couldn't.

By mid-October I'd been inside for over two months and was starting to understand all too well the unstable paranoia of rural vigilantes. I began watching the infomercials for Proactiv, the product that boasts it cures even the most severe acne, as if they were episodic television. I listened, rapt, as people told stories about their battles with skin problems and how they were now a thing of the past. I just wanted to hear other people talk about how much they hated their skin.

As luck would have it, the one person I saw every day also struggled with his skin. Claude had come to my door between three and four in the afternoon, every single day for the last sixty-three days, always yelling, "Happy Cottage Chinese Restaurant! Hello, my friend!" and waving his hand in a wide loop as if he were washing an enormous, invisible window. "Ten dollars eighty-five cent! Thank you!"

At which point, I handed him money, and he handed me the stapled paper bag. Claude was in his mid-twenties, with pronounced, curvy cheekbones and a hairdo that made me think he was a big Elvis fan. He was part of a subculture with whom I now felt an intense bond, people with skin problems, enthusiastic acne covering most of his face. Often Claude was the only person I saw all day. He was the one who noticed when I added rice to my diet, and a month later broth. "You add soup! Good for cold weather! You go, girl!" Claude said, shaking my hand. He knew more about my diet than even my own family.

Recently, in some sort of masochistic frenzy, I'd begun playing music I'd listened to compulsively after Josh and I broke up. My favorite albums were *The Globe Sessions* by Sheryl Crow and *When the Pawn . . .* by Fiona Apple, both about painful breakups and both of which I had heard described as "suicidal vagina music."

Sometimes my voice would crack as I sang along with Sheryl or Fiona, all the while thinking, "See how much I've changed! Can't you see that, Josh?" I was singing when Claude came to deliver my daily meal. I opened the door dressed in my pajamas, a ribbed black tank top and gauzy drawstring pants. He waved, smiling.

"Hello, my friend!" he said. "Ten dollars eighty-five cent! Thank you!"

I handed him the money, and he handed me my paper bag, but then he added something new.

"You singer?" he asked.

"Me? A singer?" I said, barely able to contain my thrill, as singing was something to which I'd always secretly aspired. Clearly what I lacked in vocal training, I made up for with ragged emotion.

"Oh boy, no. No! I'm not a singer. I'm a writer." I scribbled in the air just in case he didn't understand. "But thank you. That's so sweet."

"So you not singer?" he said.

I shook my head.

"So you marry?" he asked.

For a moment I thought he was just curious, until I realized his whole demeanor had changed. He seemed younger and more confident.

He continued. "You singer? I singer too!" He showed me his wedding finger. "Nothing. We two singer," he announced.

He pointed to himself, and I thought he was going to reach for my hand, but he didn't.

"Claude," I said, painfully. "I just broke up with my boyfriend. Broke up," I explained. I looked as if I were pantomiming an old Houdini trick, my hands slowly bending an imaginary metal beam. "We are broken, me and my boyfriend. I am sad."

There was a long silence before he said, "Okay!" He smiled anyway. "Okay, my friend. Okay! Good-bye!"

"Bye, Claude," I called after him, but I didn't think he heard me as he raced away, choosing to take the stairs for the first time in over two months. Claude never came back. The next day another man arrived. And someone else the day after that. And I remember thinking: "I can't believe it—now my deliveryman broke up with me too?"

I THOUGHT I'D get more used to being alone, but I was wrong. By the end of October, I started researching the mental and physical effects of solitary confinement. I would go to websites that had barbed wire around the text, often decrying the practice as inhumane. I found out that in certain studies, solitary confinement induced hallucinations, hyperresponsivity to external stimuli (which would explain how excited I got every day for my one meal), and massive free-floating anxiety (that sounded familiar). It's not often that I've thought, "What do I have in common with someone held in solitary at San Quentin Prison?" but at that point I knew exactly. And as far as torture went, I was an expert, relentlessly looking at photos of the ten days Josh and I spent in Paris.

Our first night, we went to a famous brasserie where we were seated so far away from the other diners, our waiter got winded making the journey across the room. We sat at our lonely table, giggling and sniffing our armpits, asking each other, "Do we smell?" In the following days, we encountered patisserie employees who we were convinced had spit on our croissants, salespeople who would have rather endured a colonoscopy than find us a size, and even a hostile policeman, who, upon seeing our picnic in the park, ordered us to "get off sa griss!" Every snub delighted us more. We came up with the theory that Paris is the city for lovers specifically because the contempt couples experience bonds them so deeply. We were convinced that if the French had been even the tiniest bit less disgusted by us, or tried in any way to conceal their hatred, we wouldn't have had nearly as much fun. We couldn't wait to come back.

Looking at photos from our Paris trip, I knew I was like a former cocaine addict staring lovingly at photos of Bolivia. Confined to my apartment, it was hard to resist.

One of the other symptoms of isolation was constantly thinking about morbidity, which might explain why I'd started having dreams about my mother again. Cruel ones, where she was still healthy and vibrant, even laughing. I wondered if my mother would have said one of her usual lines, "He'll be back" or "You're better off without him," in reference to Josh. Would she have told me to stay in TV or try something new? Whatever she would have said, I knew she would have made me feel better. I knew she would have said that even with the rash I looked beautiful, and brought over teddy bears with bows around their necks and cards that said, "I'm on Team You!" I still couldn't believe she was gone.

I'd been trying to remember my mother before she got sick, something that had been hard for me for a long time. I would lie on my bed with ice packs on my face and just think about her. I thought about the time we went to Japan together when I was thirteen. We stayed at a small, prim hotel in Kyoto, which boasted rooms that were completely white: rugs, furniture, lamps, towels. White. And of all places, this was the place where I got my first period. I'd woken up, and there it was—a huge stain on the sheets, as if I'd driven over roadkill in my sleep.

"They're going to know!" I wept, pointing to it.

"Who?" my mother asked.

"The housekeepers!"

"Oh, no, they'll just think you were drinking tomato juice in bed and it spilled. If you want, we can even order some tomato juice from room service, and we can leave the empty glass by the bed. Happy?"

I flailed my arms.

"No, they won't," I said. "They'll know what it is! They'll know I bled all over their sheets."

There was a knock at the door.

"It's them!" I yelled.

"Oh sweetheart, trust me. You'll see. This happens all the time."

There was another knock.

"Tell them to come back later," I screamed.

"Like, when? We're leaving in four days." She took my hand. "I'll take care of it. You'll see. Have a little faith in me. Come on."

I went to the door and let in the two older Japanese women, who seemed to speak less than no English. They seemed baffled by "hello." We all walked back into the main area, where my mother was now sitting on my bed, her hand resting next to the stain.

She smiled. They smiled and waved. "Silly me," she said. "Oh look. I must have hemorrhaged in my sleep."

I would replay this memory in my head over and over, trying to stop the other more painful ones that crept into my mind, the ones where she was in the hospital. Her brain tumor had gotten much worse by this point, and her mind was deteriorating rapidly. Once when I went to see her, she seemed confused as to who I was.

"It's me," I said. "It's Amy."

"I know it's you," she said, although I wasn't sure if I believed her. "Did my sister call?"

Her sister had been dead for over a year.

"Nope," I said. "How are you feeling, Mom?"

"What's your phone number?" she said. Only months before, she'd called me several times a day, every day. I started to tell her when she said, "Wait. Give me a pen."

"Seven-five-nine," I said.

"Seven-five-nine," she repeated, writing down a three, a six, and a circle.

I tried again. "Seven-five-nine."

"Seven-five-nine," she said, and this time she scribbled something that looked like a tangled string. She looked over at me. "Why are you crying?" she said.

"I'm not," I lied, patting down my face with my sleeve.

And then, in what I thought might be a rare moment of lucidity, she said, "Boy, you need a vacation." I managed to stay twenty minutes, writing down my phone number and leaving it by her bed.

It had been over a year since my mother died, and I thought I'd done most of my grieving, but now I wasn't so sure. There were still so many things I didn't seem to be able to accept. She'd met Josh, sort of. She couldn't speak, but her eyes were open and I thought, okay, at least my mother met my future husband. And then when Josh left, it brought back all those feelings of "she'll never see me get married" and "she'll never meet my children."

I started thinking about pain; specifically, after you feel pain, where does it go? Do you store it in your body, like fat, or expel it, like sweat? I remember Eve telling me that one time, after a painful breakup, she'd gone to a woman for "body work." This woman massaged her back and said that it was full of "implants," which she called "pockets of pain that will remain there for life." She said you could learn how to deal with the implants, even to ignore them, but they were as much a part of one's body as an arm or even a face. Maybe this rash was here to stay—my scarlet letter.

I thought about how much I used to love being my mother's daughter and how proud I was of our relationship, especially after my teenage years, during which I'm fairly sure she weighed the pros and cons of murdering me. Sure, people said that even though she was dead I'd always be her daughter, and that was true; but it was different now. I thought about all the things I wished we'd done. I remembered, just after my mother died, thinking that grief isn't only mourning the person you lost, but all the fantasies of the life you'd share, which made me think about Josh and how much I loved being his girlfriend and all the fantasies I had about our life together, and our cute kids, who would have moppy shag cuts and a room in our loft where they could play the drums.

. . .

I'D ALWAYS BEEN one to define myself by the men I was with. It was so much easier than having to think about who I was without them. In high school I was Cliff's girlfriend. After college I was David's girlfriend. In my twenties, I thought I was being so independent by seeking out a career, but it just turned into yet another thing I could say about myself. I'm a screenwriter. Now I'm a sitcom writer. I remember once Josh and I went to a dinner party and no one spoke to us until I said I wrote for TV. I remember thinking, "Five minutes ago you thought I was a nobody, but now you think I'm something," completely ignoring the part where I felt like a nobody or asking myself why.

I thought if I could just add more titles to my list—wife, mother, executive producer, Emmy winner—I could outrun my questions about myself. I started to think I was like the house in *Poltergeist,* which looked fine on the outside but was later found to be erected on a shaky burial ground, which caused it to be haunted and overrun by ghosts.

As for my face, while I never thought of myself as a great beauty, I based a lot on feeling attractive. And now I'd lost that too. I didn't even look like myself anymore. It's such a strange feeling not to recognize your own face. "Who am I now?" I often wondered. It was a question I realized I'd asked myself so many times throughout my life.

When I was sixteen, I gained close to forty pounds in a little over three months, the result of my first real breakup. I went from an awkward teenager to an unbearably awkward and brokenhearted teenager. I became convinced my ass did not merely protrude, but looked more like a shelf on which to place things like a large potted palm or a set of encyclopedias. I figured if I couldn't be pretty, I'd look as if I didn't want to be, like one of those enormous, proud lesbians with a shaggy mullet and a boundless flannel shirt, the kind of woman who always smiled politely when someone called her "mister." I started wearing butcher's aprons with combat boots, as if I were ready to either invade Poland or sling hash. I got a gender-bending, "shaved on one side, long on the other" haircut, the kind of bad eighties hairstyle some people considered even more dangerous to the world than Soviet aggression. My mother tried hard to be supportive.

"I think your outfits are . . ." She struggled to find the right word. "Very à la mode, which contrary to popular belief does not only mean with ice cream on top, but is French for 'of the fashion.' Who else but you could get away with wearing a pillowcase as a headdress? How fun!" Then she leaned in and whispered, "Sweetheart, tell me honestly, are you on pot?"

My father was far less delighted by my outfits. "Is Ringling Brothers in town?" he said.

"I'm expressing myself," I said, rolling my eyes.

"What are you trying to say? I'm a clown?"

What I couldn't explain to either of them was that I was hoping my new look could say more about me than I could about myself. My leopard fez and floor-length dashiki would say that I was a wildly inventive, deeply tortured iconoclast, who was also lots of fun. I dreamed of being adopted by madcap transvestite models and graffiti artists with trust funds. I didn't know it at the time, but this would be the first of my many attempts at reinvention, each one promising a far better life than the one I was leading. For a while, it seemed, I was willing to be anybody else, as long as it wasn't me. In college, after a brief Madonna phase, I tried "nature womyn," subsisting on crunchy stir-frys and not shaving my legs, so that from the knee down I looked like a flokati rug. Each time, I thought, "Maybe this is me," and each time I realized, sadly, it wasn't. I thought that I'd finally accepted myself. At twenty-five. At thirty. At thirty-three. But now I realized nothing could be further from the truth.

Now I'd lost everything that I thought made me who I was, and what was I left with? I had no idea. It was almost like a bad science fiction movie where you have no face or identifying characteristics. And that's when it occurred to me that although I had no idea of what was ahead for me, although I often felt these days that I knew very little if anything, I knew, with complete certainty, that this would be my biggest reinvention of all.

· 3 ·

HEARTBREAKER

My sophomore year of high school my mother announced that she had made plans for me to go to Italy.

"I'm taking you out of school for the week," she said.

"Oh my God," I said. "Fantastic. When are we going?"

"Not we," she corrected. "You're going with your father."

"Are you insane?" I said. "No way."

It wasn't that I didn't like my father; it was more that he was a stranger to me. He imported ladies' handbags and traveled constantly, going to the Philippines and Korea for months at a time to oversee production, making sure multiple pockets zipped and pudgy straw daisies were sewn on correctly. I was always hopping up and down in front of him when he returned, trying to elicit praise for something I'd made him, like a bagel necklace that said "My name is Murray" in strawberry cream cheese, or books I wrote and illustrated featuring a child meant to look exactly like me, books with subtle titles like *Look! Look! I'm Over Here!*

I was lying on my bed when my mother gave me the news. I had just woken up from my afternoon nap, which usually took place shortly before my evening nap. "I'm not going," I told her. "But nice try."

My mother was standing above me, her hands on her hips.

"You are going," she said. "Here."

She held out a greeting card with sparrows painted in slate and red ink, with Chinese writing underneath. It said: "You cannot prevent the birds of sadness from passing over your head, but you can prevent their making a nest in your hair."

"A nest in your hair?" I said. "Gross."

She rattled the card. "Look inside."

It was a note from my geometry teacher, a nice, older Polish woman who wore a different babushka every day.

The note began: "I'm worried about your daughter. Amy always seemed like such an upbeat girl with lots of friends, but recently something has changed. She seems so sad all the time, and it often appears as if it takes a tremendous effort for her not to cry when answering a question in class. I'm hoping everything is okay at home because I was concerned maybe someone had died."

The question about whether someone had died struck me as very perceptive, since, in my mind, someone had. It all began when my boyfriend Cliff went off to college and, soon after, my best friend, Beth, the girl with whom I spent my every free minute, found a boyfriend of her own. It seemed as if every time I called, Beth and her new boyfriend were crafting macramé bong holders or making falafel or having sex while listening to Brian Eno bootleg tapes. They even started to look alike, donning parachute pants and getting mullets that, in humid weather, made them look as if they were wearing Daniel Boone hats. I grew increasingly isolated, and as I did, I grew increasingly depressed.

Hoping to find people who felt as miserable as I did, I started volunteering for charities that helped famine victims in Africa. Soon I became so immersed in the world's suffering that I became completely insufferable. I managed to alienate my remaining friends by saying things like "I don't know if I can go on a ski trip to Vermont when people are starving in Africa." I was worried that a week with my father might make me feel even worse, but I didn't want to tell my mother that, and so I said, "I just want to go on record and say that this is so fucked up. None of my other friends have to go to Italy with their parents!"

"Duly noted," my mother said. "Get your passport."

. . .

MY FATHER AND I got to the airport three hours early, which, I would soon discover, was late for him. Sitting there with nothing to do, I stared at him in a way I never had before. In profile, his nose leapt out from between his eyebrows, curving into what looked like a ripe fig surrounded by nostrils. In photographs, my grandmother used to have his nose airbrushed to look small and straight. My father wore large, square glasses, and his wavy, light brown hair was cut short. Tonight he was in a long, belted raincoat, beige dress slacks, and simple, buckled loafers, which needed to be resoled, worn down by all the anxious pacing he did worrying about his business.

"So, what? You wanna get something to eat?" he said.

I shrugged.

"Yoo-hoo? You in there?" he said, lifting his hands to his ears and wiggling his fingers. "You want something to eat?"

I clicked my tongue and jerked my head to one side. "Well, yeah, God. We have to do something. We have three hours, which I could have used at home."

"To do what?" he said. "You can take a nap here."

We walked to a bright, lively cafeteria, which was crowded with people choosing from flaccid sandwiches and salads that were almost as depressed as I was.

"You want a roast beef platter?" my father said.

"I don't eat meat," I said, staring at the floor. "I haven't for, like, years."

He rolled his eyes. "She doesn't eat meat. Okay, what about chicken?"

"Just get something yourself. Okay?"

"What about stuffed cabbage? Do you like that? Or look, there's navy bean soup or red Jell-O with fruit, how about that?"

I folded my arms over my "Free Nelson Mandela" T-shirt.

"I just look at all this extravagance, and I can't help thinking about all the people who are starving in Africa."

"Since when did Jell-O become an extravagance? I ate it when I had the gout," he said, but I could tell he was thinking, "Jesus, I have to spend a week with this kid?"

The nightly news was playing on a television set, which was chained to the ceiling. As usual, the top story was footage of the American hostages in Iran.

"Uch, I know how they feel," I mumbled.

"Okay, listen, you," my father said, pointing his finger an inch from my nose. "I've had enough. This was Mom's idea, and I don't know if she was right either, but I've had it."

We barely exchanged a word for the next two hours. Or on the eight-hour flight. Or during our first day in Rome, when both of us were desperately aware that we were as foreign to each other as to the city we were visiting. Since my father was in Italy looking for Gucci handbags to copy into cheaper versions, I was on my own during the day. The hotel arranged for me to join a group tour that was going to see the Sistine Chapel.

"We were in the chapel for, like, five minutes and then they made us leave and then the bus dumped me in the middle of nowhere," I said at dinner that night. "And then I was chased by these drug addicts who were throwing flour at people, and I ran into a store and they called a cab for me. I'm going to complain. That bus company is the worst. It was dangerous."

Again, the finger came out. "You're not going to say anything," my father said. "Those companies are run by the government, and if they get mad at us, they could make life very difficult. You got that?"

"What are they going to do, arrest us?"

"You know what? You made it home okay, so leave it alone. Eat your spaghetti and stop making so much trouble."

I glared at him. I wanted to say something profound. Something about how hurt I was and how I wished he cared more about me and the fact that I'd been chased by drug addicts, but all I managed to say, through clenched teeth, was "It's not spaghetti. It's"—I hissed—"fettucini."

THE NEXT NIGHT, we went to a restaurant that was said to have the best fish in the entire city. It was very crowded, with people waiting near the door and groups of seven offering to sit at tables for four. The restaurant had the feeling of a well-lit cave: dark stone walls and low-slung ceilings. But the main attraction was definitely the buffet, which was a fountain of grilled shrimp, mussels marinara, oysters on ice, vegetables swimming in basil and fragrant oil, and robust, earthy pastas.

There wasn't even a menu. Instead, the waiter announced when it was your time for the buffet, so that each table didn't have to rush through a line. Since I'd heard it was the most popular restaurant in Rome, I'd worn my best outfit: gold, round-toed shoes with a stacked heel, my pink sweater with the beefy shoulder pads, and a Hawaiian print miniskirt. My father moved quickly through the buffet and returned to our table, while I took my time. I looked at the clams oreganata, the pesto octopus, and finally reached to the top of the fountain for some lemon asparagus. That's when I heard the clapping. It took a few seconds for me to realize I was standing in my underwear—plain, white briefs, what some people called "granny panties"—and that my skirt was now around my ankles.

"*Buon Anno!*" someone yelled, which I would later find out meant "Happy New Year." After I pulled up my skirt, I stood there laughing, and I looked over at my father, and he was laughing too, doubled over and holding his stomach.

"I look up—" He was laughing so hard he was turning red, and he couldn't finish his sentence. "And there you were in your underwear!"

I hadn't laughed that much in a long time, and I couldn't ever remember laughing with him. We laughed even more, and someone sent us a bottle of wine and a pink rose.

"You can have the flower," my father said. "I'll take the wine." He poured a little in a glass. "Okay, I'll give you a sip."

And I don't know if it was the laughing or the wine, but that night I ended up telling him how much I missed Cliff.

“You two were inseparable,” he said. “He was your nippy.”

“My nippy?”

“Your security blanket,” he said. “You were Frick and Frack.”

Then I talked about how Beth had disappeared.

“Well, sweetheart,” he said. “Get used to it, because girls will always dump you for boys. Especially if they’re having sex. Then you’re out. That’s life.”

The next night we talked about how depressed I was, and he told me how depressed he’d been after his first marriage failed. He told me things I’d never known about him. He liked cold showers every day and spent years wondering what to do with his life.

After that, I would always describe that trip to Italy as the first time I got to know my father. But this isn’t one of those stories where everything was delightful and we got along beautifully after Italy. Instead, for years after that, we simply felt more comfortable being ourselves. I learned that when you go to a coffee shop with my father, the minute the food arrives, he says, “Finish up. These ladies live on tips.”

“But the plate is steaming,” I’d say.

“Why do you have to be so difficult?” he’d say. “These people need to make a living.”

We argued when I made him a book for his birthday. It was called *The Adventures of Murray,* and I had taken weeks to illustrate it with drawings of him.

“I don’t get it,” he said.

“What’s to get?” I said. “It’s a gift.”

"I just think you've done better things."

"But it's a gift. Why couldn't you just say thank you?"

"You wouldn't want me to lie to you, would you?"

"Yes, please. Absolutely. Every day. You can start now."

Our relationship remained contentious, and we fought often, but never more than when my mother was dying. Rarely a day went by when my father and I did not argue about something. It was not uncommon to find us simmering outside my mother's hospital room, yelling in whispers.

"They're very angry at you at the nurses' station," my father informed me one morning. "That nurse over there"—he pointed to a woman in her late fifties with oversized square glasses and very long, coarse, gray pigtails—"showed it to me in the nurses' log in big black letters: PATIENT'S DAUGHTER WOULDN'T LEAVE."

"I didn't want to leave Mom alone," I said. "She was in pain and no one was giving her anything. I wouldn't leave until she was better. How can you not think that's a good thing?"

"Listen, you! Stop making trouble! I've had enough!"

And even though I said things like "My mother has a brain tumor, and I'm being left with a lunatic," my father and I were deeply fused, spending every weekend together, linked by the understanding that we were both losing the person we considered our significant other.

"Hol and Tom have their families," he said, referring to my older, married brother and sister. "But we've just got us."

And he was right. We were like one of those old bickering

couples who never stop fighting but couldn't exist without each other.

WHEN MY MOTHER was still in the hospital, my father became consumed by the idea of my meeting a doctor.

"I think it's a wonderful idea," my father announced. "But if you meet a doctor, he's not going to appreciate you complaining about the hospital all the time like usual. I mean, some of these doctors are very arrogant, and they won't appreciate you telling them what to do or how to treat Mom. You don't want to come off as too controlling, which you do a lot."

It was typical of my father to give me very specific and often insulting advice on hypothetical situations. "When you do meet a doctor," he said, "he's not going to like all that messy clutter you have in your tub, and he's going to want to eat something other than chicken."

"Mom would be so thrilled if you met a doctor," my sister agreed, and for a moment, it seemed she was imagining me winking impishly at my wedding guests as I walked down the aisle in a dress she found way too revealing in the bosom.

"She'd be delighted," my father said, his faraway look suggesting that he was imagining the same event. My father had told me for the last five years that when he jogged around the reservoir every morning, he practiced the speech he was going to give at my wedding. "But, come on, I'd like to recite the fucking thing already. I mean, I know the goddamn thing by heart!"

And when I did meet someone, no one was happier than my father.

I met Josh Adler at a dark, crowded birthday party in Soho. My mother had just stopped recognizing who I was, and this was the first party I'd been to in as long as I could remember. Josh walked in five minutes before I was planning to leave. He had wispy, black hair and tiny glasses perched atop his slender nose. He wore a black agnès b. bomber jacket, Levi's, and sneakers.

"You'll either love Josh or think he's gay," my friend Mia had told me. "But not because he acts gay. It's more that he hasn't had a girlfriend in a really long—" She exhaled loudly. "Okay, as far as I know he's never had a girlfriend, and he dresses really well, so people just assume."

Josh seemed cute and utterly harmless. He smiled a lot and was quick to laugh or point at me and say "Ha ha! Nice one!" when I tried to be funny. He talked about his long hours as a film editor. "This is the kind of goofy, sweet guy who would never hurt me," I remember thinking.

For our first few dates, I wasn't sure what I thought of Josh, and I often thought about ending things, until he stood me up one Saturday night a few weeks later.

"I don't need this shit!" I yelled into the phone when he called the next morning.

I knew that I was trying to get rid of Josh before he got rid of me. I'd long been aware that I had a fertile abandonment complex, perhaps because my mother was always getting sick when I was growing up. I'd often joked that my fear of being deserted ranked with that of someone who'd been left in a bassinet on a church doorstep.

"I wasn't getting a vibe that you were into hanging out," Josh said in his mellow, jazz cat way.

"A vibe? A vibe? What is this, 1972? Are you going to pick me up in your Gremlin? We had plans and you know it. I'm thirty-one years old! Do you know how old that is? That's old and I don't need this shit and don't you ever call me again!"

And then he begged me to meet him for brunch, saying that I should just give him a chance to prove how much he liked me. Over the next few months, I think I started falling as much in love with being out in the world again as I was with Josh. I was so thrilled just to lie around Josh's cramped apartment watching Godard's *Week End* and ordering in chicken kebab platters. Sometimes on Saturday mornings we'd sit outside a coffee shop called La Bonbonniere, sharing a plate of bacon and trying to pick out the people we thought were walking funny due to rough sex the night before. And then there was the time Josh ran out of the shower, out his front door, completely naked and covered in soapy lather, down the hall, and past a row of apartments, just to say good-bye to me before I went to work. He followed me all the way to the elevator bank, saying, "I thought I'd kiss you again before you left."

"You know, technically this is considered streaking," I said, wiping lather off my wool ski cap.

"Ha ha! Nice one!" he said, kissing me again. "Ah! Fuck! I hear someone coming!" And he ran off.

During the many years I didn't have a boyfriend, I was one of those people who would see a couple barely linking hands and think "Jesus, get a room already!" And now, of course, I was the worst. People used words like "wildly affectionate" and "all over each other" to describe how Josh and I were together. Others used more vivid phrases like "Cut that shit out. It's really annoying."

Six months into our being together, my mother died. At her funeral, a family friend pointed to Josh, saying, "I'm just so glad you have him. I've rarely seen a mother and daughter so close. We were all so worried you'd fall apart. When's the wedding?" I'd made it known that I was wondering the same thing. I dropped subtle hints like "I need to know. Are we getting married or not?" Josh always said "yes," but his expression reminded me of someone who'd just gotten kicked in the balls. And while he felt trapped, I felt that I was too much, that the events in my life were more than he could handle, and so I decided to try not to need anything. I felt as if I started out as an origami bird, one of those simple swans, but I just kept folding myself smaller and smaller, until I was this unrecognizable, crumpled wad of paper. But as hard as I tried to make myself tiny, it was still too much for Josh, he announced, right before he broke up with me.

As I WAS marinating in the kind of pain the truly wronged believe to be uniquely their own, the kind that makes you define the world as "people who have compared themselves to Job and people who haven't," I took some comfort in knowing there was another person who felt the agony of my breakup almost as much as I did.

"Fuck him! He's meaningless! A nothing!" my father said. His arms were outstretched so that his hands, which he shook with each word for maximum effect, dangled inches from my face. "You've got to forget him!" he said. "Please, sweetheart. Can you do that?"

"I still love him," I said, putting my face in my sleeve.

We were sitting at Barney Greengrass, which specialized in things like schmaltz herring and salted kippers, a modest place with the kind of bold lighting particular to certain Jewish delis and Soviet interrogation rooms. The decor was cramped, with narrow tables and rigid, wooden chairs.

"Ame, could you just look at me for a minute?" my father said, tapping my shoulder. He spoke with the sort of loud, concerned voice you might use to rouse someone who'd just fainted. "Just lift your head off the table for one moment and then I promise—promise—you can put it down again."

I sat up slowly, looking at the bagels we'd ordered with ice cream scoops of egg salad and tuna, both of which remained untouched.

"Things are going to get better!" my father said.

"Why do you think that?" I said.

"Why? Why?" he said. "Because!"

An older woman, a blonde with a frantic perm and a low-cut

pink, fuzzy sweater, batted her eyes at my father. "The tuna is excellent," she said.

"We come for the bagels," he said.

It was not uncommon for women to flirt with my father. Now, over a year since my mother's death, he had only recently consented to meeting women with names like Pearl Hyman and Gay Solomon. His new social life was reflected in his dress, which he treated with more attention, pairing, as he did today, a bright, crewneck sweater with khakis that, unlike the ones he used to wear, were not tattered along the edge and stained with bits of Bloody Mary mix from his evening cocktail. My father's dates, mostly widows, often sported silky hair teased into virtual pillbox hats. They were all very nice and charitably active, but as my father would say after each one, "She's no Mom."

And now, the two of us, both single, met daily.

"That woman is flirting with you," I said.

He looked at the woman, who kept fluttering her eyelids and pursing her rouged lips. "I don't give a shit about her," he said. "I care about you. Sweetheart, please, let me just tell you one thing. I think it'll cheer you up. Ready?" he asked, excitedly.

I nodded. This was the first breakup my father had ever handled, and I was eager to hear what he had to say.

"You know Mom got kicked around by lots of men, dumped left and right by every Tom, Dick, and Harry, before she met me," he said brightly. "Just like you!"

I looked at him. "This is going to cheer me up?"

"I'm getting to that. After Mom got divorced, she traveled

around Europe on a moped with a Bulgarian. I think it was either a Bulgarian or a Rumanian and maybe even a few others. She was all over the place. She was a mess. Anyway, then she came back to New York, and I know for a fact she went out with at least one alcoholic and then a producer who two-timed her and some editor from the Associated Press."

When my mother was alive, my father often referred to what he imagined was her lively single life before she met him, to which she replied, "Thanks, pal. I had one boyfriend, and you make it sound like I was running a brothel."

He continued. "What I'm saying is your mom found me. And you'll find someone too."

"So will you," I said.

It just came flying out, and if I'd had another moment, I probably would have chosen a different response. Now we were both single? It was all very weird because it was all so new.

"We're not talking about me," he said. "Don't drag me into this. Keep me out. You want to know why this happened? You really want the answer?"

"Yes. I would really like to know why this happened."

"Because you didn't really want to marry Josh." He slapped the table, folded his arms, and nodded his head once. This was the answer.

"You're wrong," I said. "I wanted it very much."

"You might think that's what you wanted," my father said. "But you're gonna realize you didn't really want it at all."

After all the years of being my father's daughter, I was very familiar with his three-card-monte approach to psychology, which said, essentially, no matter how much you think you know something, you don't, because reality, while a fine concept, can never really be trusted.

"Maybe," I said. "But the fact is I would have married Josh and thought I was happy, and now everyone's telling me I wouldn't have actually been happy but only thought I was happy because I wouldn't have known how deeply unhappy I really was. But if you don't know how unhappy you are, doesn't that mean you're happy?"

He looked at me with confusion that bordered on pain.

"Y'know what?" he finally said. "You got lucky. You hear me? Lucky. You dodged a bullet. Now, your job situation, that's a different story. That I can't say is so lucky because you're unemployed and so you've got all this time on your hands, which I can understand. It's the worst."

Recently, my father had made the difficult decision to retire. When he was caring for my mother, he drastically cut his work schedule so he could spend every day searching Gourmet Garage for soups he thought she might like and sit by her bed telling her how beautiful she was, even though she was bald and her face was paralyzed on one side. After all that, he had tried to put his business back on track, but it was too late.

"That's why you need a profession and not just a career," he explained. "See, if I were a lawyer, I could be working now, I'd be thrilled. I could go into the office a couple of days a week like Martin Sidelitz and help detained Africans, but you can't run a bag business that way. Keep that in mind when you figure out what you're going to do next."

He looked at me to see if I was following his line of thinking.

"Sweetheart, we're very depressed, aren't we?" he asked.

"We are." I nodded. "And really, really anxious."

"I'm going to repeat what I said, and you should listen to me for once and not be so goddamn stubborn. Please. You're better off without him."

I wasn't sure if I agreed, but believing I was lucky seemed to cheer him up, so I let him think it was true.

IT WAS NOW June, and I was still no closer to any sort of peace. Because all of my friends worked and it was hard for them to find a three-hour window in their day to answer the teary question "How can you say you're in love one week and just freak out the next?"—the task of taking care of me fell to my father. This was something I'd never expected, as only a year before I had considered it my duty to take care of him. Often when Josh and I were out to dinner or seeing a hot new deejay from India, I would duck out to call my father, my heart breaking a little when he said he was sitting alone watching a documentary about Albert Speer and picking at a stale roast beef sandwich.

This was before he announced he was ready to meet someone. When he did, his only request was that each woman be over sixty. "I wouldn't have anything to say to someone younger. I mean, what do I have to say to a child of fifty-six?" Immediately, he was offered not a handful of names, but enough women to comprise an all-female tabernacle choir. Twice.

"What am I supposed to do with all these?" he said, placing a new list of names in his growing pile. "I feel bad, but there are just too many!"

While Manhattan was scarce on affordable apartments and parking spaces, it was, apparently, filled with older widows and comely divorcées, many of whom hoped to convince my father to choose them. As a result, it was not uncommon to visit his apartment only to have the doorman call up to say, "A lady just left a Bundt cake downstairs." Or to have a neighbor who was almost eighty send flirtatious letters written in girlish script, promising to invite him over for her famous Wiener schnitzel as soon as she returned from vacationing with her great-grandchildren in Austria.

I was nervous about my father meeting someone. I'd had a friend whose father, upon remarrying, removed all of his former wife's pictures from the walls and the family albums. But I also knew that my father needed to be taken care of. When my mother first got sick, he didn't know how to order Chinese food over the phone. "Do I call and say number sixteen or do I say the Double Happiness Shrimp? What do people do?" All the times I'd argued with my father, it never occurred to me how helpless he was. I was always so aware of his enormous effect on me, I never imagined that one day he would need to be taught how to turn on the stove and scramble an egg. Or that I would search his cupboards to make sure he had something in the refrigerator besides Spanish olives and an old rind of Edam cheese. Or that I would have to write down two pages of directions on how to work the VCR, directions that began "Press the ON button."

I knew that a part of me wanted my father to meet someone, so I would feel less responsible for him. And so I took to regularly quizzing him about his two or three dates a week.

"Okay, so her husband died of a heart attack and you took her to Lusardi's for dinner, but do you like her?" I asked eagerly. "Will you take her out again? Maybe you should give her another chance."

"I don't know," he explained. "She's a nice lady, but we've only been out twice, and she's asking me if I want to escort her to her nephew's Bar Mitzvah in Cincinnati."

He appeared to be struggling with his decision. "Ame, it's not as simple as you think."

"I know it's not that simple," I said. "Remember all the times you asked me why I didn't go out with someone a second time?"

"Don't be a wiseass. And while we're on the subject, Greta Garbo, it's time you started dating."

"I'm not ready."

"She's not ready." He shook his head. "Nipplehead, you're a

beautiful young lady. You're intelligent. You're kind. Forget that schmuck and get out of the house. Because, if you don't, it becomes a kind of a syndrome, don't you think?"

"A syndrome?" I asked. This reminded me of the time he told me if I didn't clean out the cat litter, the fumes could make me go blind.

"Like an obsessive thing," he said. "It's time."

"I'll think about it."

"Are you bullshitting me?"

"I'm not bullshitting you."

"Because we've always been honest with each other, so don't start bullshitting me now."

"I'm not bullshitting you. I'll think about it. Now leave me alone."

Which I knew was a ridiculous request because we could no sooner leave each other alone than stop breathing.

Several months later, my sister called after dropping her son off at tennis camp to tell me she had good news.

"Mandy Simon's husband, Mitchell, who you met last year at Sports Authority—remember he was carrying the red plastic kayak? Anyway, twenty-five years ago he was a counselor at a camp and he's still friends with one of the boys who was in his bunk, and he wants to fix you up with him. And wait! Before you say no, I told Mitchell you would say no, but he said this guy never accepts blind dates and we're lucky he said yes."

She was winded by the time she finished.

"Plus," she added, still catching her breath, "your rash is clearing up, so you have no excuse."

"Fine," I said. "I'll go."

"No? Wait. Are you being sarcastic? Really?"

"Yeah. I'll go. Whatever."

"Okay, his name is Aaron Ungerleider," she said, rushing off the phone before I could change my mind.

I TOOK MY father to see a movie called *Happiness,* which featured, among other things, an obscene phone caller who ejaculates onto his wall.

"What are you trying to do, kill me?" my father said as we left the movie theater.

We decided to go to his new apartment, the smaller one he had gotten a few months after my mother died. Our plan was to order in pizza and watch TV. My sister had decorated his new den with earthy colors that were both masculine and warm. It was more elegant than the apartment my parents had shared, in part because my mother, feeling sorry for her only unmarried friend, Eden Levine, had let her help decorate, even though Eden's tastes ran to life-sized ceramic tigers, sugary pastels, and anything wicker. There were a few pieces that had been taken from my parents' old apartment: the blue floral sofas; the Chinese celadon lamps; the bizarre art my mother loved to collect, professing her fascination with the grotesque. But now these pieces seemed lost. Surrounded by so many framed pictures of my mother on every shelf, they seemed to be asking, "Where is she?"

After we ordered dinner, my father looked at me, beaming until he couldn't hold it in any longer. "Your sister told me you have a date!" he said.

"Word travels fast," I said. "Yes. Next Monday."

"Finally, the Eagle has landed!" he said.

Once again, I was reminded of how much had changed. Years ago, I would have responded to his excitement with a curt "Calm down" or "I don't want to talk about it," never imagining one day I would want him to meet someone as much as I knew he now dreamed of it for me.

"Dad, it's just a dinner."

"But don't you see?" he said. "One date will lead to another date and another. When the men of this city find out you're available, it's going to be a bonanza!" As he'd already used a term from the Old West, he felt comfortable throwing in another. "A stampede!"

He assumed that because he was given lists of women, I would be offered dozens of men keen on wooing me. The reality was just the opposite. Often when talking to people who said they knew of someone they might want to introduce me to, I felt as if I were campaigning on behalf of myself, trying to show them why I was the right candidate for the job. "He's the greatest guy, and he'd be perfect for you, but he lives in L.A." might be followed by my saying, "I would move for the right person!" I tried to explain to my father that it wasn't the same for me; I didn't get long lists of potential suitors, far from it, but he refused to believe me.

"Bullshit! When the men of this city find out you're available, you'll be beating them off with a stick! You're such a pretty girl." Suddenly, his look of elation turned very serious. "But I'm going to give you some very important advice. Are you listening?"

I nodded cautiously. "Maybe."

"Everyone asks me, 'Why is Amy single?—' "

"Everyone asks why I'm single?" I repeated, horrified. "Who asks why I'm single?"

"Who asks? Well, lots of people," he said, appearing to be computing the large number in his head, giving up only when he realized a calculator was necessary. "The Berkowitzes asked. Pat. Arlene and Milt Sussman. Hy Gittner—"

"The guy who used to sell handbags in your showroom asked why I'm still single?"

"They don't mean it in a bad way. They don't say"—he furrowed his brow—" 'Why is Amy single?' No, they say it like"—he smiled—" 'Why is Amy single?' It's a compliment. I tell everyone it doesn't make any sense to me either, I don't know what happened, but can I make a suggestion?"

"Do you have to?"

"You need to wear your hair like this," he said, laying his palm against the gray and brown curls that framed his sun-spotted forehead. "Away from your face. Not the way you're wearing it now," he said pointing to my long hair. "When you wear it all messy, it looks like animal fur or a nest or something. You're a beautiful girl, but no one can tell if you wear your hair that way."

My father had a penchant for simultaneously complimenting and insulting me, saying things like "Ame, you look terrific! Thank God you're not wearing that furry hat. It was so ugly. It scared people away."

"You don't really think the way I wear my hair is the reason I'm not married, do you?"

My father continued to clutch his front curls in a fist. "If you wear your hair like this, I guarantee you will meet someone and it will last." He smiled. "I'm just so delighted you're dating again. You're going to meet someone very soon, sweetheart. You know why?"

"Why?" I asked, genuinely interested.

He sunk his right hand onto the top of my head, as if he were crowning me something. "You used to be such a pain in the ass, but look at you now."

THESE EXCHANGES LEFT me confused, and not only for the obvious reasons. It was strange to realize that if my mother hadn't died, my father and I would never have become this close, never would have had this relationship I'd always wanted. When my mother was alive, she acted as the mediator between me and my father. If I had a problem with him or he with me, it was always channeled through my mother, who went to great lengths to explain us to each other. "Your father needs control," she might say. Or "Amy needs to feel she's being heard." My whole life I craved my father's attention, and now I was getting it. When people admired how close my father and I had become since my mother's death, I didn't know how to explain that I felt as if I had lost my mother and found my father. It had never occurred to me that joy could be as unnerving as pain, that you would wrestle with why something good had happened the way you might struggle with something terrible. And yet now I found myself trying to understand both.

AARON UNGERLEIDER WAS a tall expert on the Middle East. We met at a sports bar with exposed brick walls and murky lighting. He was good-looking, in what Eve called the "Al Gore, clean-cut, every grandmother in Florida thinks he's handsome sort of way."

"You told me to look for a girl in a brown shirt," he said. "That's maroon. That's not brown."

"It's chocolate brown," I said, but what I was really thinking was "One drink and I'm out of here."

"Relax," he said, slapping me on the arm. "Just a little blind date humor. You know, like when you tell someone over the phone that you're a bald, obese midget in a wheelchair."

After that night, Aaron called me constantly, often several times a day. Once he even called me from an airplane. He invited me over to watch *Reservoir Dogs* while he did laundry. Another time he called and said, "I'm thinking about you. Let's get some Korean." I wasn't sure if I liked him, but I knew I loved the attention. Soon I began to warm to him. And then I never heard from him again.

"Baseball still hasn't called you?" my father asked when we met for lunch. He called him "Baseball" because I'd told him Aaron, who had once considered playing professionally, now played in a local league. "Did you sleep with Baseball?"

"Dad!"

"You're not a nun. You're not Sister Amy Cohen. I'm not asking for details, but if you slept with him this is going to be much more painful."

"No," I said. "I did not sleep with Baseball. I only knew him two weeks."

"Well, maybe Baseball got tired of waiting," he said. "Tell me what happened."

"I don't know. He acted like he liked me, he talked about our future plans, but it was this fake kind of intimacy. You just realize that what seems like intimacy can be so deceptive."

"I've got a great story for you," he said, smiling. "When Mom and I started dating, she had a bust out to here!" he said, straightening his arms away from his chest. "She really filled out a sweater. And then a couple of months later we were at her apartment and I saw all these big socks on the floor, and I realized that she wore falsies." He was beaming now. "Is that what you mean by deceptive?"

"Not exactly," I said. "It's more like when you think you're getting close to someone but then you realize you're not as close as you think you are, that they're just telling you things to make you feel close. Like when people talk about things that seem intimate and special, things they say they would never tell anyone else, but then you realize it doesn't mean you're actually any closer. Does that make any sense?"

I caught a look of despair from across the table.

"You don't tell this to men on dates? Do you?"

WHILE I WAS recovering from the Baseball debacle, my father went out constantly. My friends and I marveled at his social schedule.

"Jesus, the man is popular," my friend Eve said. "It's like he has groupies, except instead of waiting in his hotel suite naked they bake him Bundt cakes." Eve had just broken up with her boyfriend of several years and had herself reluctantly begun dating. "I mean, I have to stand on one foot and hop up and down just so I can get introduced to some business dweeb who tells me I'm high maintenance because I go to three chiropractors."

"Can you believe it?" I said. "It's his fourth date this week. And he could have three times that many if he wanted to. We all need to be reincarnated as an older Jewish man with an apartment on the Upper East Side."

"Exactly," she said. "No one's leaving me Bundt cakes in the lobby."

When I would tell my father this, he would say, "Ame, these ladies are just so relieved I'm not in a chair and I can remember their names. I get bonus points for just being able to walk to the restaurant without an attendant."

If he wasn't taking a blunt divorcée to a movie or escorting my friend's husband's mother's neighbor to a Haydn concert, he could always be found with his lonely, unmarried daughter. In fact, we now spent so much time together, so many days and nights, when people would ask if I was dating again I would often answer, "Apparently I'm dating my father."

We were watching television in his den, as we did now every Sunday night.

"Lemme ask you something," he said. "When I call a lady for the first time, should I leave a message on her answering service or not?"

"Why not," I said. "That way you hear each other's voice once before you talk, and it doesn't feel as much like an ambush."

He thought about it for a moment. "Well, I think you're one hundred percent wrong. That's not very smart. What kind of cockamamie advice is that?"

Somehow I wasn't surprised. Often, giving my father advice felt like handing an ice pick to a toddler, as it would, undoubtedly, be used against you.

"I like to speak to a lady directly because what if, like me, the lady doesn't know what buttons to push to work her answering service? Then I'll be sitting around waiting for her to figure it out and that could take weeks, and I'd be left to twiddle my thumbs, wondering if she got the message or not. Who needs that?"

"Then don't do it."

"I won't," he said. "Sometimes your advice isn't so smart."

We sat in silence, watching a sluggish documentary about Sacco and Vanzetti. Ten minutes later my father turned to me. "You really think I should leave a message? Maybe you're right. If you like to hear a fella's voice first, maybe one of these ladies would too. What the hell. I'll try it. Thanks, sweetheart."

In early March, my father and I attended a lecture given by John McCain at a community center on the Upper East Side. The crowd, thick and slow moving, was comprised mostly of men and women wearing heavy wool sweaters in eighty-degree weather. For the over-sixty-five crowd, this was the equivalent of Woodstock. And while there wasn't free love, there was free food, our exit clogged by people stuffing packaged sandwich cookies into their bags and downing cups of free grape juice. This is why we were virtually at a standstill when we heard someone yell, "Murray!" from across the room.

We turned around to see a woman whom I imagined to be in her early seventies moving toward us, each step followed by a brief but noticeable pause. She wore an elegant red suit woven with gold thread and had calves so thin they looked as if broom handles were rising out of her suede-tipped Ferragamo shoes.

"Hello, Murray," she said in a throaty voice. By the way she was straining to maintain her composure, I could tell she had gone on a date with my father and that he had never called her again. I knew this look myself, the look that said, "I'm devastated, but I'm going to pretend not to care that you didn't want me. Asshole."

As she stared at him, her eyes pleading, I knew she was now hoping he would give her another shot. She looked at my father as if he were a serum that could save her life.

"Esther," he said warmly, and from the way he said it I knew she didn't have a chance.

She knew it too.

"So nice to see you, Murray. Is this your daughter?" she said, trying to sound very cheerful, what was called "gay" in her era, before it meant leather chaps and rainbow flags.

"How had this happened?" she seemed to be asking as she smiled at me. She had organized her life specifically, done all the right things, married the right person, so this would never happen. I wanted to tell her I knew how she felt. Life was full of meteors. I didn't understand anything myself. How could Josh, a man I loved so much, a man whose apartment I scrubbed after his friends, who were in a band modeled after Phish, came to visit and told us they spent the whole time jerking off in his bed and watching porn. A man I laughed with all the time. How could he leave me? And here we were, Esther and I, both afraid, wondering whether to blame the stars or ourselves.

“She seemed nice,” I said as we left. “Are you sure you don’t want to go out with her again?”

“Ame, she’s a lovely, just a lovely, lovely lady, but not for me,” he said. He sounded upset about it, as if he wished things could be different.

“I think you should give her a chance,” I said, and as I did, I realized that, in some magical way, I was hoping if I could convince him to give her another chance, I might get one myself.

“That’s the woman I told you about who broke her hip getting off the escalator at the opera. She slipped on a mint or something.” He stopped for a moment. “Life’s not fair sometimes.”

Even though we were forty years apart, biology had left both Esther and me vulnerable. It had left her a widow, as it had so many women who survived their husbands, and it had left me anxious to meet someone, as I hoped to have a baby within the next few years. I assumed that as a teenager, Esther, like me, had felt she had the upper hand, and now we were reduced to this. Just thinking about it made me annoyed at my father.

“All you care about is looks,” I said.

He shrugged. “Hey, I didn’t choose this. I’d rather have Mom. You don’t want me to be alone for the rest of my life. Do you?”

SINCE I’D ANNOUNCED to my friends and family that I was ready to try dating again, the response resembled a well-manned telethon where unsuspecting men were hit up not for donations, but dates. I said yes to anyone who asked. I went out with a guy who told me, as we were waiting on line at a crowded trattoria on Houston, "I haven't had sex in six weeks, and it's making me really edgy." And a man who pretended to be blind so he could bring his dog on the subway. And an investment banker who took me to dinner, where we talked about our shared admiration for seventies disaster movies, before he asked how many men I'd slept with and did I own a vibrator.

One night, my sister, Holly, called to apologize for giving my number to a friend without telling me. I had been taken completely by surprise when a man's tentative voice began the conversation with "Hi, this is Teddy Shandling. Teddy Shandling?" he repeated. "Your sister's friend's husband works in an office with my friend's wife. I think."

"I'm so sorry," she said. "I thought I told you."

"I mean, how could you? It was so embarrassing."

"It won't happen again. I promise but, more importantly, what do you think about Dad's girlfriend?"

"What girlfriend?"

"He didn't tell you he has a girlfriend?" She sounded shocked. "You two spend so much time together."

"Yeah, well, he told me he's been on a few dates with this one woman, who recently took a trip to Sedona, but no. He didn't call her his girlfriend."

She made a sound, not quite a laugh, that suggested she too was starting to understand our father in a new way.

"It's so funny. Ever since you and Josh broke up, he's been saying to me, 'I hope Amy meets someone first. I hope Amy meets someone first.' Maybe that's why he didn't tell you."

"Yeah, maybe," I said.

The following day I met my father in front of Saks to buy him a new suit.

"What's wrong?" he asked. "You seem, you know . . ." He tried to think of the right word. "Upset about something."

My mind was racing. "Nothing," I said, but what I was really wondering was "Why didn't he confide in me?"

"Are you sure you're okay?" he asked.

"Yeah," I said, and we headed upstairs.

Later we went to lunch at the Saks cafe, which overlooked Rockefeller Center on one side, complete with a roof garden, and St. Patrick's Cathedral on the other.

Trying to make conversation, I told my father the vibrator story.

"He really asked you that?"

"I said if he wanted a vibrator so much he should get his own."

"Well, I think you should have stood up, grabbed your coat, and said, 'You may talk to other young women that way, but I don't care for that sort of behavior. Good night, sir!' "

Apparently my father thought my date took place in 1953.

"Ame, you gotta weed out the guys who just want to get in your pants," he explained.

"Could you, please?" I said, pressing my hand in the air to signal him to lower his voice.

"You think anyone here is so interested in your sex life? They couldn't care less."

He took a bite of Cobb salad between sentences, spearing a cube of Canadian bacon. "Now, a lot of men are going to hear that you haven't had a boyfriend for a long time and think, 'She's been on the schnide,' " he said, using his term for lack of sexual activity. "They might think, 'It's going to be easy to go to bed with her, because she's desperate—' "

"On the schnide?" I said, annoyed.

"Can I make my point, please? Please?"

"Go ahead."

"What I'm telling you is, you can't let that happen, because you need someone who's going to be good to you and take care of you. You're very special. You're much stronger than I thought. You used to be such a pain in the ass. Oh, you drove me nuts, but you haven't had such an easy time lately." He looked closer. "But your skin is looking better. Anyway, any young man would be very fortunate to get you. So don't forget that. Capeesh?"

At that moment, I remember feeling lucky, but guilty that we'd only found each other this way because my mother died. And then it occurred to me that maybe that's how my father felt. Lucky, but guilty that he had found someone first.

I thought back to when were sitting at that restaurant in

Rome and he told me that people would always dump you for someone else if they were having sex. I wondered if that's what would happen to us now. I wondered if we would begin arguing the way we used to. Or if he would just slowly disappear. Or if maybe, just maybe, he would surprise me.

· 4 ·

THE LATE BLOOMER'S REVOLUTION

When I was growing up, my family ate dinner together every night and discussed the news of the day. That's why, in 1975, at age nine, I knew that Saigon had fallen and the Vietnam War was finally coming to an end; New York City was in a serious fiscal crisis and in danger of going broke; and the three most powerful people in the world were American president Gerald Ford, Russian leader Leonid Brezhnev, and Mindy Weinstein.

By all accounts, Mindy Weinstein was not only the most popular girl in our third-grade class, but in the entire elementary school. She was lithe and blond, blessed with a rare button nose that was adorable but also possessed character. Legend had it that sleeping at the Weinstein house was nothing short of paradise: a mason jar overflowed with candy, and unlike at my home, where bedtime resembled lights-out at Attica, bedtime at Mindy's was merely a helpful hint. Annie Ferrara said that when she slept over, the whole family made shrunken apple head dolls, dressing up empty Windex bottles in clothes that Mrs. Weinstein sewed herself. But Mindy was not content to be merely the best student, athlete, or most well-liked girl in our class; she wanted to write. And that's where I came in, providing the Magic Marker illustrations for her first book, about an enormously popular girl and her friends, who are good at everything and all live happily ever after.

The book was an enormous success, reread twice at Show and Tell. I was convinced this was how I came to be invited to Mindy Weinstein's birthday celebration, a bicycle riding party in Central Park, the first Saturday in May. Each girl was instructed to bring her bike, as "a bunch o' lunch" would be provided by Dr. and Mrs. Weinstein for Mindy's "Birdle Daydle Doodle." I was delighted to be invited. So delighted, in fact, that I neglected to mention one tiny detail: I didn't actually know how to ride a bicycle. But I wasn't worried; everyone said it was the easiest thing in the world to do—I expected to be doing wheelies by noon.

Boy, was I wrong.

"Oh, my God! Amy! Are you okay?" Dr. Weinstein asked, jumping over the woven plastic fence through which I had just crashed. "Can you say your name? Can you hear me?"

I nodded, still a bit stunned. I was lying on my back, a few inches from a sign that said "Keep off the grass!" Dr. Weinstein came toward me, his hands outstretched in anticipation of broken bones.

"I'm fine," I said, praying that my small accident had not been as public as it felt.

"She's okay! She's okay!" Dr. Weinstein yelled over to a crowd of people who had rushed to the scene. "Thank you all very much, all of you! You can all go now, she's fine!"

"I really don't know what happened," I said. "I told my parents to get this fixed. It must be because I ride it constantly."

I sat up. My elbows were bloody and my pants were ripped, but I knew that neither of these things compared to the real damage. Mindy stood with her arms folded, looking forlorn, her head bowed, as Mrs. Weinstein tried to comfort her. From my place in the mud, I could see the other girls, ten in all, waiting, gripping their handlebars. They looked, I thought, like the tribe of restless Apaches I had once seen in a Western, a long line of warriors poised for attack, hungry to burn log cabins and scalp people. I knew immediately I would be their story Monday morning. "Gahd," they would tell the other kids. "She can't even ride a bike."

My standing with these girls was iffy. I worried they thought I was a dummy, because I was in the slowest reading and math groups, and weird, because of things like the recent Show and Tell incident.

We had been told to find out who our most famous relative

was and give a short presentation in front of class the next day. I was worried. The only even remotely famous relative I knew of had dressed as a dog with glasses at a theme park in Florida before he gained fifty pounds and entered a cult. I went home and asked my mother if she could think of anyone better to mention, and she informed me, to my delight and surprise, that we were closely related to someone extremely famous.

The next morning, all the kids stood at the blackboard. Evan went first, excitedly telling us all that his second cousin was none other than "Fonzie," which elicited "oohs" and "ahhs" from the entire class. Lizby's grandfather helped invent antifreeze, which got a "cool" from one of the boys. And then it was my turn. We were being graded on presentation, and I was careful to speak clearly and slowly and to stand very straight, with my hands folded neatly in front.

"My mother told me," I announced proudly, "that my most famous relative is Moses."

"What a dumbass," I heard someone say in the back of the room.

Not surprisingly, at lunch when everyone hovered around Evan begging for an autograph from The Fonz, no one asked me for an autograph from my most famous relative, perhaps worrying that the stone tablets would be too heavy.

Now Mrs. Weinstein removed her tennis visor and yelled, "Ben! Is she okay?" She glanced at her watch and then looked back at us, annoyed. "I mean, do we need to call an ambulance?"

Dr. Weinstein waved his hand above his head. "Go on!" he

called back, at which point all the kids yelled "yay!" and took off.

"We'll meet them for lunch in Sheep's Meadow," he explained.

"I can still ride," I said, stepping onto my bike. "We can catch up to them!"

"No!" he shouted. Worrying he had scared me, he added calmly, "No. It's such a nice day. Let's walk."

As we pushed our bicycles up a steep hill, I considered explaining to Dr. Weinstein that my mother had been struggling with her second bout of breast cancer in three years, and the reason I didn't know how to ride a bike, when my brother and sister rode perfectly, was that there was too much else going on in our house. But since I had just told him that my favorite book was a collection of Diane Arbus's photographs, her transvestite series in particular, I thought I'd said enough.

Two hours later at lunch, as the other girls compared stories of dodging a carriage pulled by a horse wearing a straw hat, I tried to make conversation. "Wanna see my rip? Wanna see my bloody elbows?" I asked, but the girls looked up only briefly, and then with scant enthusiasm. That was the last time I ever got on a bicycle.

Until today.

WHEN JOSH AND I were still together, he could be heard on many weekend mornings saying, "I wish we could go bicycle riding today because it's one of my favorite things, but, yeah, well, I guess we can't." He had since moved on and moved in with his new girlfriend. I had neither moved on nor moved in. Instead, I decided to buy a bicycle.

Today I was at the Bike n' Hike, in Hampton Bays, Long Island. The store was housed in a small, white cottage with green trim. It needed a fresh coat of paint. If someone were to write a book about Heidi in her later years, as a heavyset, older Swiss shut-in, still wearing her hair in braids and yodeling to no one, she might live here.

"So, Amy, what can I do you for," a man named Leon said, wiping grease on his red and puce tie-dyed T-shirt. He was all smiles, with just enough teeth to chew small cubes of beef without choking. "Are you looking for a road bike? A mountain bike? What?"

We were standing behind the house, in a narrow backyard, which was paved with cement. Growing up in Manhattan, I've had a long-standing relationship, dare I say a love affair, with concrete. I referred to the balding patches of grass in Central Park as "nature." I appreciated the miles of sidewalk that make New York the walking city that it is. But now, as I imagined myself on a bicycle on this same cement, my feelings changed. I imagined nasty scrapes. Gushing blood. Head injuries. Flash cards reteaching me the alphabet.

"Leon, I haven't been on a bike in a really long time," I said.

"A really long time like what? A year, five years?" he asked.

"More like twenty-five," I said.

"Really?" he said. "Get the fuck out of here. That's a riot."

"Wait till you see me ride," I said. "Then you'll really have a laugh."

He readjusted his long, gray hair, letting it first fall down his back before gathering it into a ponytail. "Better late than never," he said. "That's what I always say. Like, last year I took a stand-up comedy class. I'm fifty-three, but I thought: what the fuck, Rodney Dangerfield started in his forties and people tell me I'm as funny as Leno, right?"

"Absolutely," I said.

Leon patted me on the back. "So, what made you finally learn to ride a bike?"

"Ah, you know, it seemed like a good thing to do." I was going to say something about how nice the weather had been or how a bicycle was the perfect way to see the beach, but I already felt a bond with Leon, so I decided to tell him the truth. "My boyfriend broke up with me."

"Wow, that's rough," he said. "Recently?"

"No. A year ago," I said, realizing that twelve months had gone by. I had that odd feeling where it seemed as if everything had changed in my life, but also nothing at all. "So, here I am. Empowering myself."

"Jesus, well, you don't look lit up or nothing." He elbowed me. "Get it? Lit up? Empowering! I'm just kidding. Anyway, Amy, seriously, what kinda bike you got in mind?"

"Big," I said. "I want a big bike that basically rides me." I spotted a model that looked perfect. "Hey, what about that one?"

"That?" he said. "That's a kiddie bike. I was just about to put a banana seat and bell on that."

He wheeled out a heavy, copper-colored number that was essentially a Barcalounger on wheels. The frame was thick and sturdy, the width of a heavy, kosher salami. To my delight, the seat on the bicycle was huge, like a cushion you would sit on after extensive hemorrhoid surgery.

"Whaddya think?" he said. "This baby's seat is almost as big as my ex-wife's." He punched me in the shoulder. "See. Everyone's got exes."

"Listen, I'd love a seat bigger than your ex-wife's, trust me," I said. "But I need it lower."

"Amy, it's practically a sled."

"I would just feel better if my feet could touch the ground."

"Your feet okay, but not your knees!" he said.

A group of people had congregated, all waiting for Leon to help them. There was a stony-faced couple who seemed dressed not for a ride around Long Island, but the Tour de France, in tight, yellow spandex outfits that said "Cinzano" in several places and little paper caps that resembled the ones cafeteria workers wear. They stood next to a woman whose fidgety son pointed to me and asked, "Mommy, Mommy, why is that lady taking so long? She's taking too long!"

He threw a rock at a squirrel.

The woman, who was wearing a loose jacket made of hemp, knelt down next to her son, and immediately I could tell she was an explainer. "Sweetheart," she said. "We can't throw rocks at squirrels because the squirrel doesn't like it. See how fast it's hobbling up the tree. It's scared and it wants to cry. You wouldn't like it if someone threw a rock at you, would you?"

He threw another one.

"Amy, try this out," Leon said, tapping the seat. "I'll hold on to the back."

"Great," I said, nodding a little too rapidly.

Standing there, I had no idea of what to do—pedal, then push off? Push off, then pedal? I was lost. Not knowing the simplest steps to riding a bicycle led me to think about all the other things I'd assumed I'd know at thirty-five, but didn't. I liked to consider myself a late bloomer, meaning someone who would eventually, however late, come into bloom. Although when and if I would bloom remained a mystery. I wished I knew how to speak a foreign language fluently. I had always fantasized about being able to argue in Italian, flailing my hands over my head while yelling "Basta! Paolo!" I wished I knew how to cook a simple roast chicken well or that I had read *The Brothers Karamazov* or *The Idiot,* whose main character sounds like someone I could relate to. I mentioned this to a friend, telling her that I often felt overwhelmed by all the things I didn't know, to which she replied, "Don't know anything? Don't know anything?" Her tone was enthusiastic and cheerful. "You've been in therapy forever. You know so much about yourself!"

"Okay, Amy, I can tell you're freaked out," Leon said. "I'll hold on to the front and the back and jog alongside you. Better? We'll go up and down right along here."

He motioned ahead to a short path, which led to the picket fence of the house next door. He didn't understand that these few feet were terrifying to me. I considered the picket fence, and the words "call 9-1-1!" and "she's impaled!" came to mind. I took a deep breath. And then another. And another. In a second I was going to need a paper bag.

Leon took hold of the bike. "Ready, Amy?"

"Mommy, that lady's hands are shaking," the little boy said. "They're like Grandpa's hands."

I looked down at my hands, trying to steady them unsuccessfully. I read somewhere that the only reason people have trouble learning things when they're older is they have more fears and complexes. Part of what led me to the bike store this morning was my great desire to be less afraid. I was determined to take more chances. I had often thought that if I had to choose a slogan to describe my approach to life, it would be "I fear, therefore I am." As a child, I was always the kid who wore a life preserver just to dangle my feet in the shallow end. I thought about a guy I dated recently, a correspondent for the BBC. When I asked him when he had been afraid in his life, he paused, touching the short beard he had grown on assignment in Afghanistan. "Well, I suppose it was when we entered Somalia as the Americans were arriving and our van got caught in a firefight between dueling warlords." His voice was chatty—he had used the same tone when describing how much he liked the soft pretzels at Coney Island. "That or when I got shot in Kosovo," he added.

"Leon," I finally managed to say. "Leon, Leon. I need a moment."

My sister, Holly, and her seven-year-old son, Eric, arrived. They had just bought him a new helmet. I wondered if someday I'd ride as well as my seven-year-old nephew. He had just gotten his training wheels off.

"How's it going?" she said.

"Leon has the patience of a saint," I said. I moved closer to her so I could whisper. "Listen, I'm going to put the bike in the back of the car and learn to ride it when we get home," I said. "I'll be less nervous. It'll be private. I think that's the best idea."

My sister smiled. "The car's not here. Dad left. We're riding home."

"Wait. Riding home? It's almost ten miles."

"That's the only way you'll learn," she said.

"On the highway?" I said, pointing to the road in front of the Bike n' Hike. "Are you trying to get rid of me?"

"You just need to get out there," she said. "If you get Dad to pick you up, you're never going to learn."

"That's not true," I said, knowing she was absolutely right.

"Listen, I know you. You'll ride around the block tomorrow. You'll fall a couple of times and that will be it."

This was typical of our relationship. My sister pushed me; I pretended to hate it, but secretly thought it was good for me. I knew she was right, even though I didn't want to admit it.

The man in the Cinzano shirt was now poking his finger at the Explainer, whose son was kicking the skinny tires of what appeared to be an extremely expensive, custom-made Italian bicycle.

"It's not a matter of opinion," the man said. "Two plus two equals four and we were here first."

Leon turned to me.

"Honey, this mob is ready to blow. What's it gonna be?"

I regarded the picket fence in front of me and remembered crashing through the plastic barricade in Central Park twenty-five years ago. I thought about all the times Josh suggested a bike ride and I had to say no.

"I'll take it," I said.

Soon Leon was saying, "Careful out there! Don't break anything!" I laughed loudly, and then, when he wasn't looking, secured the strap on my helmet.

My sister and her son were already so far ahead I couldn't see them anymore. I was standing at a traffic light debating whether to walk across the wide intersection toward the Shell station on the opposite corner or attempt to ride. I was joined by a heavy couple in their fifties, who, I imagined, had recently met with a cardiologist who said if they didn't get a little exercise soon, they'd both be dead within a year. The man was wearing shiny warm-up pants, white loafers, and a gold pinky ring. The woman had a piled black bouffant—more durable than my helmet—that looked as if it weighed almost as much as her bike. What I loved about them was that they seemed as thrilled as I was just to be riding at all. I felt as if they understood the pedal, pedal, push mentality. The woman turned to me and said, in a voice that only a lifetime of smoking could produce, "Gorgeous day, right?" And for a moment, I felt as if the three of us were struggling together. That is until the light turned green and they glided forward without me. A minivan slowed to let me pass; the driver, honking gently, waved her hand to let me know she was giving me the right of way. I smiled and then, panicking, pantomimed a cramped leg, shaking my foot wildly. I even grabbed my calf and began massaging. It was not pretty, especially when I realized no one was even watching. When the minivan was long gone, I jogged my bike across the road.

I began to worry that I might not make it home—that buying this bike was a stupid idea. I worried I'd made a huge mistake when I decided to stay in New York and take a break from television writing. I had a career and a direction and now what did I have? Grease smears all over my inner thighs. I worried I'd never fall in love again. And even as cars honked at me and I actually did have something to worry about—namely getting called "a fucking idiot!" one more time—I told myself not to give in to my fears and the voice that said, "You're too chicken for this."

I thought about what I wanted to change in my life. I wanted to change the way I spoke to myself. I wanted to start talking to myself like one of those iconic football coaches who say, "You can win this! You can do anything!" Which led me to ask, as I often did, how much can you change about yourself after a certain age? I mean, really change. Can you go from being a pessimist to an optimist? From a wallflower to a ballsy broad? It's often taken for granted that your early years and teens are essentially a dress rehearsal for the rest of your life. If you do well, you're on your way to a great performance; if you do badly, don't worry, it's not the real show. Recently, I'd even heard people refer to their twenties as part of their youth, as in "I got married when I was twenty-three. I was just a kid." But it's often assumed that by your thirties, you are who you are. I found that interesting since I felt as if I only really started growing up at thirty-one. My mother's cancer and subsequent death played a big part. My whole life she called me her "little girl." I think the younger she treated me, the younger it made her feel, and I was happy to oblige. It was only when she got sick and allowed me to take care of her, when her stroke turned her mind into that of a child, that I became an adult.

This was the kind of thing I thought about as I rode. I remembered something my friend Ray told me when I said I finally wanted to learn how to ride a bike. He was a mountain biker who loved to point out the raised scars on his legs and explain how he got them. "I got that one when I missed a turn and went down a hill when I was riding in the woods at midnight. And I got this one when I hit a barbed-wire fence riding in the woods at midnight."

He looked down at his legs, regarding his wounds.

"Not to get all Buddha and shit on you, but I like the whole idea that if you look too far ahead or too far behind you'll crash. You have to find the right balance on a bicycle or you'll fuck your shit up."

I pedaled now, trying to look just ahead of me. I was trying to stay in the bike lane, or at least in the vicinity of the bike lane. To my great surprise, I was actually moving; unsteadily, yes—my handlebars were jerking sharply left, then right. And before I knew it, I was down. On the ground. On my ass.

"Are you okay?" my sister said, riding up.

"I am," I said, slapping the dust off my pants. "Although I think I might have broken my ass."

She helped me up. "Ame, when you ride, you have to stay within the white line or it's really dangerous," she said. She pointed to a thick painted dividing line, calling attention to the generous area between it and the sidewalk.

"Stay within the line?" I said. "I'm trying to stay within New York State."

She looked across the intersection at her son, who was riding in circles. "He's dying to go. Honestly, will you be okay?"

"Of course I will," I said. "And besides, I can always walk. After all, it's only ten miles."

"Just stay within the line. I'll keep checking on you," she said and rode off.

"See you in six to eight hours," I yelled after her.

I passed a tony petting zoo where children named "Ainsley" and "Trip" petted goats that were checked daily for mange. Farther down the road, I went by a market that sold cartons of seven-dollar orange juice. My skills had improved slightly in the last hour, and I was able to do three wheel revolutions before I lost my balance and threw my feet to the ground. My hip was throbbing from my fall, and in addition, I had wide, spongy blisters on my palms from clutching the handlebars so tightly.

One of the things that led me to consider bike riding was that for the past year I'd taught "spinning" classes part-time. Teaching spinning, which uses stationary bicycles to simulate a rigorous ride outdoors, was not as easy as I'd imagined, less physically than because you had to field questions like "Amy, instead of playing 'Sympathy for the Devil' during the warm-up, could you play my daughter's version of 'Somewhere Over the Rainbow'? She's nine. We sent her tape to Ben Vereen, and he loved it!" Then there were all the times I felt compelled to lie, like when a group of orthodontists asked my advice about their forty-mile bike trip upstate to see the foliage. And while I never exactly said I had done it, I did say, "It's a great ride," never mentioning that my experience was from the inside of a car.

In any case, all the spinning had made my legs very strong—not lean; I don't come from lean people. I come from Russian women whose ankles were even thicker than their mustaches and who welcomed wearing eight skirts in summer. "You are strong, you can do this," I told myself as I careened toward a parked Mercedes convertible.

A young woman in a crocheted bikini top and acid-washed jean shorts emerged from the front seat. She studied her fender.

"Um, you hit our car," she said, thickly. "And we weren't even moving."

She rubbed her long nail, done in a pale French manicure, along the tiny scratch. "This was, like, totally brand-new," she said.

Once again I was on the ground. My second time in less than an hour. I must have taken quite a spill, because now my water bottle was smashed in half, and I was lying in a pit of gravel next to a set of active railroad tracks.

"I'm so sorry," I said. I realized my helmet was askew, halfway off my head actually, and my pants, stretchy and black, were covered with dirt and had big rips, as if they'd been chewed along the bottom.

The man at the wheel had a waxy chest and wore a ropy gold chain around his neck, a dollar sign scattered with small diamonds, which swayed as he spoke. "Forget it," he said. "Let's go."

I was still gathering myself: my helmet, the remains of my bottle. I stood slowly, lifting up my brand-new, gigantic bike with its enormous seat.

"No way," she said. "It's scratched."

He widened his eyes and jerked his head toward me. For a moment she seemed confused, until she looked closer, and suddenly her contempt turned to sympathy.

"Are you okay?" she yelled, articulating each word dramatically. "Are you alone?"

I was wondering if there was a group home nearby and they thought I'd wandered off.

"I'm fine," I said. "Thank you."

She got into the front seat of the convertible. "Well, you just be careful because"—she pointed to a car passing—"this is a busy road. With lots of cars. So stay within the white lines."

The young, attractive couple drove off, nuzzling, as I sat picking bits of gravel out of my underwear.

It occurred to me that I had literally been in this same position twenty-five years ago. It occurred to me I would never be Mindy Weinstein, the girl for whom things came easily. I'd heard Mindy was a local prosecutor with two children. I, on the other hand, was single, unemployed, and lying in a ditch. I got back on my bicycle. And almost immediately I fell off. I had seven miles to go, and I was limping, but already I knew that tomorrow I would get on this bike again. I would pantomime my cramped leg. I would let people think what they would. Maybe I would work up to being able to go ten wheel revolutions before falling off, all the while telling myself, "Forward. Just go forward."

· 5 ·

MÉNAGE À TROIS

As far as I'm concerned, the only reason to try to look your best at all times is because when you don't, when your hair has the damp, chalky texture of someone who was buried alive, you know you're either going to run into someone from high school or, in my case, a celebrity I'd met three years before when he appeared on the television show I used to write for. John Kazan was famous, and I was not. Or not yet, as I liked to think, although now I was pretty sure my only chance for fame would be if I shot people randomly from an observation deck. John wasn't Tom Cruise famous, the kind of famous where people sell your old dry cleaning stubs on eBay, but he had a successful career as a reporter, and people knew who he was, including everybody now stepping off the elevator into the gym lobby, watching him or, like me, pretending not to watch him.

"Is that . . . ?" an older woman whispered to me in the elevator. The doors had just opened. I told her I thought it was, but I wasn't sure. His head was down again. He moved like someone who knew people were staring: hastily scribbling something on his notepad and making it seem very urgent. He nibbled the tip of his pen, and we observed him the way you might a monkey at the zoo. "Look! He's thinking! Now he's opening up his pad again!" He wrote something else. It might not have been a breaking story about arms negotiations, it might only have been a reminder about his weekly tanning session, but whatever it was, he made it look very, very important.

"It is him," a young woman with a rosy, plump face and slender glasses said as John finally lifted his head.

We all watched as he ran his fingers through his hair, which was a buttery blond (did he have highlights?) and brushed into a crisp side part. He fixed his eyes on something in the distance. It was his cut-to-commercial pose, the one where Tom Brokaw or Peter Jennings appears to be mulling over the story they just delivered: the alarming rise in nationwide shark attacks or male nurses who kill. It was the expression that said, "If there's a crisis, look no further. I'm your man."

I let everyone file out of the elevator before me. First, a tiny, pale man wearing a Knicks basketball ensemble, which hung loosely on his delicate frame, gave John the thumbs-up as he stepped into the revolving door. "Dude, take it easy, man," he called over to him. "Keep it up, yo!"

Next, the older woman standing with me in the elevator waved as if she were tinkling piano keys. "I liked your report on death row inmates with low IQs," she said. She tapped her right temple. "It made me think."

"Thank you," John said, sweetly, and his spunky nostrils flared slightly as he smiled.

She moved closer, taking dainty steps in her yoga shoes. "What do you think about what's going on in the Middle East?" she said. "It's such a shame, isn't it?"

"Uh, well," he said. "It's very complicated."

The woman moved closer. "You know, I have a single granddaughter."

His smile changed. This was the even sweeter one that meant "Not a chance."

She shrugged. "Oh, well, she would have killed me if I hadn't tried," she said, and left.

And then it was just us in the lobby. I didn't care about celebrities. I'd met lots of them, including a famous actor who offered advice to the male writers on our show. "If you really love your wife or girlfriend, I mean really love them, you have to cheat on them, because if you don't, you'll resent them. Cheating is what keeps real love alive." "Walk away," I told myself. "Take your dignity while you still think you have some. Go." But I just stood there, waiting.

John looked at me as if to ask, "You know me, but then, everyone knows me, but do I know you?"

I'd like to say that I didn't blurt out, "You don't remember me, do you?" but I did.

To which he replied, "Of course, I remember you. Hello again," he said, evenly. His manner was formal, congenial. He was so even. I was so odd. And, it seemed safe to say, getting odder.

"Are . . . ?" I said, shifting from one foot to the other. "Ouch. Shit." One of my biking cleats banged into my hip. "Do you actually belong here?"

Now my hair had twisted into thick, heavy locks, which made me look as if I played with a reggae band on weekends. Standing there, I felt myself becoming far too aware of the difference between "dewy" and "sweating uncontrollably." With any luck, John would merely assume I was going through menopause.

"I've been a member here for a while," he answered, and his eyes seemed to say, "You poor thing. You will die alone."

He was all muscle under his jeans and thin leather jacket. Later when he would tell me he had a personal fashion consultant, I imagined her convincing him to wear the round, houndstooth cap he was now putting on, which made him look, well, like he should be yelling, "Papeh! Get yer papeh heya!"

"Are you still writing for television?" he asked.

"No," I answered quickly. I didn't mention that I had just taught a spinning class upstairs, my not-so-new part-time job, or that, to my horror, during the class, I had accidentally yelled the words "feel the burn," something I'd sworn I would never say. Not even when I was alone. Not even in my head. It was a phrase I hated only slightly less than "think outside the box." I also didn't mention that I had started writing a column about dating for a weekly local paper, or that one of the pieces was titled "The Don't Touch the Vagina Monologues." I didn't say any of these things, just, "good to see you," as I waved goodbye. And that was that. Or so I thought until he called a few weeks later, and I mistook him for the exterminator.

My problems with mice began when a restaurant was remodeled on the ground floor of my apartment building. At first, I ignored the things I heard in the kitchen: the rattling of dishes, the soft shuffling of plastic bags, the thumping that sounded as if someone were performing Riverdance in my oven. I told myself it was next door—the oboe player who was always having loud sex with the windows open was probably just letting his ferrets run free—until I actually saw a mouse on my kitchen counter.

The building manager informed me that the entire complex was infested. She said the management would be happy to send the exterminator, in four to six weeks best-case scenario, because he came only once a month and would need to get to the older shut-ins in the building first, unless I insisted, in which case they could try to get to me before the housebound woman who was in traction on the second floor. I called several private exterminating companies. Which was why, when John called and all I heard was static on the other end, I said, desperately, "Hello? Is this the exterminator? My apartment is infested with mice!"

In the delicate world of first impressions, this would not have been my choice. I like to save my crazy for later. I know I'm crazy. You know I'm crazy. But we'll get to that later. Until then, look at how I can act like Princess Grace of Monaco. Or the qualities I share with Audrey Hepburn, when she was Unicef ambassador, gracefully cradling a young Somalian orphan. That's how I'd like to start things off. We can get to my psychosomatic rashes in the future. Let's say month three.

"You must think I'm nuts," I said. "Did I scare you?"

"No," he said. "Well, maybe a little bit."

"I have mice," I said. This was my way of saying, "See, I'm not really crazy, because I have an explanation, even if it's an explanation that makes me seem crazier."

"Mice," he repeated. "That's terrible." He explained that he had gotten my number from our mutual friend, Fred. "Well," he said, and waited a moment before speaking again. "Well, I was wondering if you wanted to have dinner sometime?"

"Yeah," I said, casually, having started off the conversation as crazy. I wanted to show that I could be casual too. "Let's."

He told me he was going to Washington to interview the Senate majority whip, and we made a date for the night he returned.

"You do know you're going out with a pundit," my friend Eve said. She was referring to John's occasional participation in round-table debates on weekend news programs. Eve was lying on her carpet doing yoga stretches to help relax her aching hip. She turned toward the wall, and her long blond hair trailed behind her. She was wearing chocolate velour sweatpants and lifted a plush knee up to her chest. I sat in a striped armchair, watching her.

"Must we use 'pundit'?" I said. "He prefers 'reporter.' "

"Ame," she said, soberly. "He's a pundit."

She said "pundit" with a certain disdain, as if "pimp" or "pedophile" could be substituted in its place. "There's nothing wrong with it, although, no offense, I think he could be a little less wishy-washy about global warming. I mean, he's about as intimidating as Rosalynn Carter. He should be screaming at the Republicans about breaking the Kyoto treaty, but instead, he nods and listens."

"I'll mention that," I said. "It'll be my ice breaker."

"You're so lucky you can be attracted to that kind of straightlaced, nerdy type," Eve said, now turning to face me. "It's a gift. I know millions of women find him attractive, but I never could. I need someone more, I don't know, more, more . . ." She waved her manicured hand in the air, searching for the word she was looking for. "Masculine."

"I'm trying to broaden my horizons," I said. In the past, my tastes ran to "artistic types," men who felt about settling down the way cats feel about being thrown into a full bathtub. This was the kind of thing I could say when I was being glib, that it was the men who were to blame, but the truth was, I had started to wonder if these men really didn't want to settle down, or if they just didn't want to settle down with me. With this sense came a whole new wave of insecurities: I worried that in dealing with people, men in particular, I was not letting them in or not quite showing who I was when I let things out. Or something. Something was either not getting in or coming out wrong. Basically it was an emotional import/export problem, and I wasn't sure what to do about it.

Eve sat up, interrupting her exercise routine. The E! channel was playing clips of celebrities walking into the most recent *Vanity Fair* Oscar party. We stared, slack-jawed and silent, as Catherine Zeta-Jones loped into Morton's.

"The lack of justice at the Oscars is so frightening," Eve said. "I mean, a normal-looking actress, and I'm not saying plain, I'm saying a very pretty girl could have all her teeth whittled down to stubs and gain fifty pounds, and they would say she was just doing her job. She's an actress. It's her job to create characters. But if a beautiful actress doesn't wear lipstick in one scene, they give her the Oscar. It's sick. We live in a sick, sick society."

I had started to respond when she shushed me.

"I just want to see Brad Pitt walk in," she said.

Anyone who knew Eve knew she had very definite ideas about celebrity, and so it came as no surprise that she had very definite advice for me.

"Let me just say that I agree it's flattering that the pundit asked you out," she said. "Lots of women would like to be in your shoes. I know that, but," and now she pointed her finger at me, "I think it's important for you to remember that I find him repulsive."

I smiled at her. "And I love you for it. I feel a lot less nervous now."

"Nervous! He's the one who should be nervous. You can at least debate a subject without backing down. I mean, if you bring up ways to be less reliant on foreign oil, he'll cower."

APPARENTLY, EVERYONE HAD a few thoughts about my situation. My father called the next day, a few hours before I was meeting John for dinner.

"Beverly and I are going to the theater in an hour so I need to make this quick," he said, referring to his girlfriend of two years, an elegant, sporty widow with a blond pageboy haircut. "Just remember, he's the lucky one. Not you. Him."

I reminded him that John and I hadn't even gone out yet.

"Keep an open mind. One date could lead to lots of dates," he said.

"And it could just be one," I said.

"Impossible," he said.

"Possible," I said.

I'd been on a number of horrible dates recently, which had led my father to suggest that I write something about them. "Write about all the bad things," he said. "I think it could be funny." When someone uses the words "dating life" and "funny" in the same sentence, the words "profoundly disturbing" and "in ten years I'm going to be dressing my cats in sailor suits" come to mind.

I'd always imagined that one day I would write about social injustices, but I thought that would mean hunger and poverty, not men who couldn't commit, and that's why, although I knew I was lucky to be getting paid to write these columns, I still got a little defensive about it. When asked if I wrote about dating, I would answer, "Yes, but I call it pain."

My father's pep talks had often taken on a kind of fervor bordering on hysteria. It remained a great source of anxiety for him that I wasn't married, and he seemed convinced that the right amount of coaching could do wonders.

"Okay, let me say one more thing." His voice was rising, gaining momentum with each word. "Are you listening?"

"I am."

"You sure?"

"Sure."

"If it is only one date. Then it's his fault. Not yours. You're terrific, and he's not so high and mighty. He got very flustered when that right-wing columnist challenged him about school prayer, and he'd be very, very lucky to get you. He can be very meek, and you're a beautiful, lovely person. So don't forget that."

When we got off the phone, I realized I was starting to feel like Rocky going into the ring to fight Apollo Creed. I wasn't getting ready for this date, I was being primed for it.

My sister called next to ask what I was planning to wear and if I was nervous. I told her a black, cap-sleeved Marc Jacobs

T-shirt and low-rise jeans that, if worn too low, gave me more cleavage on my ass than my chest, and yes, I was a little nervous. It had been two years since Josh, and I still didn't feel particularly comfortable on dates. Apparently, when I was told as a child not to talk to strangers, I had taken it to heart. While many people seemed to have the perception that dates were whimsical and brief, I had found the opposite to be true. It can often feel as if you're sitting next to a complete stranger on a long plane ride, except at the end of the flight, instead of escaping to someplace warm and exotic, where you lounge on a sunny beach sipping piña coladas from gouged coconuts, you just go home to your crappy, dark apartment.

JOHN SAID HE wanted to go somewhere he hadn't been before, which made me realize something I hadn't really considered. I knew some of the places he had been because I had seen photos of him in magazines and newspapers. Photos of him coming out of Lot 61 with an actress who played a forensic psychologist. Photos of him in a tuxedo at a homeless benefit, waving with a cupped hand, like Miss Universe. I suggested the Grand Mandarin in Chelsea, a choice I questioned almost immediately as we were seated under a dripping ceiling. As a result, the red pile carpet had an odor you might smell if you were trapped inside a neglected hamster cage. The only thing missing was shredded newspaper and an exercise wheel.

An older waitress with a short, boyish haircut approached

the table. She handed us two bulky menus: loose-leaf binders containing several laminated pages. Each looked like the kind of thick packet you might study to get your real estate license. John read each dish description carefully. He pored over the story of the man who inspired "General Tso's chicken," who some think might actually have been "General Ciao," named after a visiting Italian diplomat, perhaps the wannabe Marco Polo of his time. Looking at John across the table, so engrossed in the noodle section, I thought: "I didn't study this hard for my SATs." I also did terribly on my SATs, ranking with people who barely filled out their names.

"Well," he said, looking down at his binder. "Do you like spinach?"

"Yes, I do," I said. "I like spinach."

"Me too," he said. "What about the shrimp in black bean sauce and the house ginger spinach?"

He closed his menu.

"That sounds like a good choice," I said.

A friend of mine called this sort of well-mannered exchange the "Polite Olympics." "People try to out-courteous each other," she said. "They compete to see who can be more polite, and there is never any winner because you just end up feeling like a bigger and bigger loser the longer you do it."

For all the fanfare preceding this date, it was feeling a lot like any date. The substantial pauses. Each of us starting an awkward sentence and then saying, "Oh, no, you first." The discussion of summer camp. He liked it, whereas I viewed the forced canoe trips and dusty, campfire sing-alongs as a more enjoyable kind of concentration camp.

"I was always plotting ways to escape," I said.

"Yeah, I wasn't like that," he said. Rather than sounding proud, he sounded almost woeful, as if he wished he had been a little wilder growing up. "I was such a good kid."

"Mmm. Well, I wasn't."

I told him I'd grown up across the street from the Metropolitan Museum, and sometimes my friends and I would troll the fountain for loose change and use the money to buy ice cream. He told me he was always invited to the museum's galas, and I explained that I had recently given a donation myself, if only to make up for the few dollars I stole.

John talked more about his involvement with a children's charity, one that provided instruments for kids who couldn't afford them, but I didn't hear anything, as I was now hypnotized by his hair. Not the color or the cut, but instead the solidarity of it. He had what could only be called "group hair," which didn't appear to have individual strands, but instead moved and shifted as an entire unit. Even if there was spray involved, it was just so perfect. It was the kind of look I'd tried to achieve on my own hair with gels that promised, but failed, to deliver the "ultimate hold."

He asked about my mice. I told him I decided to try spackling the holes in my kitchen myself. I showed him my frayed fingertips and explained that "steel wool" is just another way of saying, "tiny, jagged wires that will rip your skin to shreds even if you wear gloves."

"You're very independent, aren't you?" he said, sounding, even in his off hours, like a man who interviewed people professionally.

"I don't think independent's the right word," I said. "Desperate's more like it."

I had forgotten this perk of eating dinner with strangers. You could portray yourself as whoever you wanted to be for the hour and usually get away with it. I could have said I was training to walk the Appalachian Trail alone. Or I spent the summer in a yurt in Nantucket. What did he know?

"But a lot of women wouldn't do the job themselves, right?" he said, managing to come off as both complimentary and chauvinistic. "What made you want to spackle it yourself? It must have been something."

Before I had time to answer that I was just too cheap to hire a professional, our pork soup dumplings arrived.

"Wow, these are great," he said, biting into a particularly chubby one. "I know they're called soup dumplings, but I was still surprised when the soup came out."

"I know what you mean," I said. "They're very juicy."

Normally, I wouldn't have thought at all about my response, dull as it was, chalking it up to first date jitters, but that was before I realized the people at the tables next to and behind us weren't talking, but instead were listening to every word we said. And boy were they getting their money's worth with our conversation.

"Wow, these're really hot," John said, fanning his mouth.

"I know. I almost burned the roof of my mouth," I said.

"Me too," he said.

"They have chicken and vegetable too, but the pork is the best kind." Okay, now I was boring myself. *The pork is the best kind?*

"The soup is good too," he said. "I didn't expect it to have so much flavor."

A bony young woman who looked as if she lived on a diet of cigarettes and Carefree gum edged her chair closer. She was the kind of woman I would have imagined with John: blond, with tan, unblemished skin and tiny feet that were wedged into tall heels. I looked down at my own feet, wedged into sandals that caused my bunions to dart out sharply, like meaty pearl onions. I had bunions. My grandmother, Grandma Flossie, also had bunions, and wore nothing but orthopedic shoes later in life. These shoes looked more like ungainly hooves than footwear, and as a result, from the knee down she often reminded me of a Clydesdale. I glanced over at the girls who were watching us. They were silent. As was the older couple on the other side of us, who looked as if they might have met through personal ads in *The New York Review of Books*; the woman wore chunky, ethnic jewelry and the man had a loose, gray afro.

"Hey," I said. "Did you read the editorial in the *Times* about the budget cuts that could threaten to eliminate school lunches for low-income children?"

"Uh. No," he said. "Do you want some spinach?"

I bit into a long, ribbony piece. I had never paid such close attention to my eating: the clacking of my teeth as I chewed; my wrist circling, idly, as I wound the leaf around and around the chopstick; the warm, oily ginger sauce landing on my chin. John didn't acknowledge that people were watching him, but I thought I noticed him lifting his spoon more carefully. He took tidy sips of broth and dabbed the corners of his mouth with his napkin. Being watched made him bolder, more confident, whereas I would have welcomed a burka.

After dinner, we walked a few blocks along Eighth Avenue in the twenties. It had rained a few hours earlier, and the streets were still slick and smelled vaguely fishy. There was no viscous fog, no dramatic wind, but it felt as if there should be. This was because I kept thinking of the kind of surreal weather used in dream sequences in certain Fellini films; the ones where Marcello Mastroianni wonders in scene after scene how far he's drifted from any self he recognizes, and here I was, walking by a bar called "The Ramrod" with a pundit.

"I have an admission," he said. "I wanted to meet the Amy Cohen who wrote the book about dating, and that's why I called."

"Really?" I said. "Well, I thought you were the exterminator. When did you realize we weren't the same person?"

"Just now," he said. "That was my way of asking if it was you."

"Oh, aha," I said. "Well, it's not. That's another Amy Cohen. I only wrote some tiny, little pieces for a newspaper about—" I hesitated, a little embarrassed. "About dating. They're about dating."

He asked me to describe them.

"Well, one was called 'Woo Is Me. The Courtship Question.' Another was called, 'It's Over? When Did We Begin?'—about people who break up with you when you didn't even know you were dating. Or when you have to break up with someone because they think you're a couple after you've had dinner twice."

He flashed me the same grin I had seen all over town on the sides of buses—ads for his morning show.

"Well, just don't write about me," he said, punching my arm gently.

I could tell I was nervous because I thought of using the word "pundit," even though it had no relevance to the conversation.

"You know, I have a reputation for never going on a second date," he said.

"So do I," I said.

He smiled. "This was fun. I think we should do it again."

The cab came and I got in. We said good-bye.

. . .

"Did the pundit wear makeup?" Eve asked, when she called later. "I'm not talking mascara. Just foundation."

"Would you stop?" I said.

"What?" she said. "It's not so far-fetched. I thought maybe he came straight from the studio, and he was still in full stage makeup. Geneva went out with a guy who's on Court TV, and she said he arrived at dinner wearing more makeup than Little Richard. It's obscene. Men call me 'high maintenance' because I get a facial every week and I like to take cabs, but it's okay if they wear pancake makeup to dinner. This world is insane."

I agreed.

She sighed. She asked if I thought there would be a second date. I said it seemed likely; he had asked, but who knew?

"I understand," she said. "I feel the same way. For me, male behavior is a lot like the Whitewater scandal. I've stopped trying to understand it."

The next morning the phone rang at seven-fifteen.

"I couldn't wait," my sister said. "How was it?"

In fairness to my sister, Holly, she usually called after every date, although this morning she was at least an hour ahead of schedule.

"Fine," I said, still trying to wake up.

"Just . . . fine?" she said.

"It was a date. He was nice."

"You need to have more fun with this," she announced,

which I took to mean "If it were me, I'd be having more fun with this."

"You're right," I said. "I'll try."

My sister's call was followed by several more throughout the day. At first, I just felt popular. All these people were dying to talk to me, I thought, until I remembered that many of these same people used to wait days to return my call. Now I was hearing what their voices sounded like when they couldn't wait to hear what I had to say. "You just went to Chinese! Really?" they said. "Did he mention meeting the pope? Or George Clooney?" They hung on every word. "What did he wear?" "Are the rumors about him being gay really true?" All of which made me wonder if any of these people had ever been interested in anything I'd ever said before or if they'd just been humoring me for the last one to thirty-five years.

On our second date, John suggested soul food in Harlem. There were no tables when we got to the restaurant, so we stood by the door waiting for something to become available. The restaurant was brightly lit, with high, beamed ceilings and creamy yellow walls, with bold paintings that depicted magnified views of tropical fruits: the fine, black whiskers of a kiwi and the mottled rind of a mango. People were looking at John. Some smiled. Others did the rapid up-and-down stare. Tonight, John had on a heavy leather jacket that made him look like an extra in a fight scene from *West Side Story*.

"I like your jacket," I said, really just to say something since it didn't look as if we were getting a table anytime soon.

"I can't take credit," he said. "My fashion consultant picked it out."

"Fashion consultant?" I said. "Is that like a personal shopper?"

"Well, yes," he said. "But she calls herself a consultant because she asks if you like something before she insists that you wear it."

"Interesting. Did she . . . ?" I said, pointing to his neatly pressed jeans.

He nodded sheepishly. "Yup. And the sweater. And the loafers. But I picked out the socks myself."

I thought about the kind of men I usually dated, who thought a formal shirt meant anything with buttons. Men who said things like "I'd rather die than wear a tie."

"I get photographed a lot," he said.

I had given a great deal of thought to what I would wear on our second date, and after great consideration, I had come up with a slight variation of the same thing I had worn on our first: a long-sleeved, black T-shirt and jeans.

"It'll just be a few more minutes, folks," the hostess announced to the line, almost ten of us now.

A woman wearing a bright dashiki with a giant sarcophagus on it looked at John as if to say, "That's right, Mr. Newsman. Mm hmm. You gotta wait in line like everybody else."

Other people whispered, "Is that him?" which was followed by "Who's she?" The difficult part about people asking who you are is that it forces you to ask yourself. What do you say to that? The answers are almost worse than the question. You either sound as if you just came from a hopped-up twelve-step meeting: "I am someone. Dammit!" Or a slow-witted *Playboy* centerfold: "I am a native New Yorker. I like to draw. I try to be nice to people." Or, in my case, a guide to working your way down the corporate ladder: "I'm a former television writer/producer who now teaches spinning part-time and writes freelance articles about dating." Or, worst of all: "I am the person who wonders often if I made the right decisions in my life. The one who wakes up at three in the morning worried it's all downhill from here."

We were finally seated. We had been at our table a little over five minutes when a husky, bald man who had let the sides of his hair grow long enough to pull into an unfortunate ponytail, a sort of dangling midlife crisis, came over to the table.

"Hey, John, you came to hear my set at the Bottom Line three years ago when I was playing with my band Noodledini and here," he said, handing him a CD. "This is my latest solo album. I just wanted you to have it."

"Does that happen to you a lot?" I asked, after the man had returned to his table.

"All the time," he said. "It's not so bad. The music is usually bad, but it doesn't bother me. What bothers me is—" He stopped, taking a bite of a honey drumstick smothered in Tabasco. "When I went to see Dave Matthews, I had to leave because so many people were coming up, wanting to talk. They would say, 'Hey, John, what do you think about the death penalty?' Or 'Do you think Bush really won the election?' With really, really famous people, sometimes they leave you alone. But with me, everyone thinks I'm their buddy. That's a drag."

"I'd hate that," I said. "I'd hate being stared at."

I was eating the Al Sharpton Plate: waffles and fried chicken, the plump meat glistening under a pool of heavy syrup.

"You get used to it," John said. "And it's not all bad. Like, it's really nice when people come up and say they like your work or that you helped them get through some terrible disease or you changed their life or something."

He used the Wash'n Dri the restaurant had provided to neatly wipe the sauce off of his fingers. This made me self-conscious about having not only licked my fingers clean a few minutes before, but also my palms and the cuff of my shirt.

He glanced around, casually, but it was clear he was looking to see if anyone was looking at him. "You know, I briefly considered becoming an actor."

"You did?" I said.

He looked genuinely surprised. "You didn't know that, really?" he said. "You haven't read anything about me?"

"No," I said, which was only partially true. Years before I had read a short piece on him in *Time*, and then there were a few items in the *Post*, but nothing substantive.

"You didn't google me after our first date?" he asked. He sounded disappointed.

It wasn't such a crazy question. In the past year, I had "googled" every man I dated. When my Aunt Jeannie called and said "Would you be interested in a furniture maker who lives in rural Maine and isn't much of talker?" I went on to the computer and found photos of his folksy rocking chairs, the kind that would be used by people who made their own cider. And clothes. I googled the Hollywood agent who told me before we'd even ordered drinks that he'd once almost taken a bath with Uma Thurman. During dinner he gazed into my eyes, saying, "Before I went to rehab, I used to only date strippers, but now I don't need to go for looks anymore." I googled the former *GQ* editor who said my living room was okay, but my bedroom looked dumpy because I kept my sweaters in plastic storage containers. When I told Eve that story, she said, "Well, that's no loss because clearly he's gay. Commenting about your plastic storage containers is like wearing rainbow suspenders and marching in Gay Pride."

I explained to John that I wanted only to know what he told me. "I specifically didn't read anything about you so we could get to know each other without any of that," I said. I presented this as a very positive move on my part, although I seemed to be the only one who felt this way.

"Oh, okay, interesting," he said, smiling. Then he held up his hand and scribbled in the air, "Check, please?"

He kissed me quickly in the cab as he dropped me off at my door. He said good night.

THE NEXT DAY John hadn't called, and of course, this was the day I knew I would see my whole family, as we were celebrating the first night of Passover at my Aunt Jeannie's house in Scarsdale.

On the drive up I told my father that John said he liked my apartment. He had seen it briefly when he'd come to pick me up.

"Oh, really?" my father said, and he seemed to be picturing my apartment, which was dark, lit by a single window that faced a narrow courtyard. It was decorated with furniture I had found at the flea market: a curly wire lamp with pink metal roses, two yellow, striped scroll-arm chairs with fraying upholstery, and some painted Moroccan tables.

"That's terrific," my father said. "If he says he likes your apartment that means he's very, very interested."

I was confused. "Why? Because he said he liked my apartment?"

"No," he said, smiling. "Because he's lying."

"Why wouldn't he like my apartment?"

"Forget about that," he said. "Listen, when I was courting your mother, I lied all the time. I told her I liked opera, the ballet, anything to make her think I was artsy. And it worked."

"So your definition of courtship is lying?"

"No," he said. "Well, maybe a little."

My aunt Jeannie, who was blond and sparrow-boned, greeted me at the door with open arms. "I heard you're dating someone we all know!" she said. She took my coat and pulled me in for a private chat.

"Pussycat, is he very bright?" she said. "He comes across like an encyclopedia on television."

She retied her silk scarf so that the knot sat perfectly on her throat, and then eased her hands into the pockets of her pleated wool trousers.

I was about to answer when my cousin Michael's wife asked where she should set up her high chairs. My aunt told her to put them at the end of the table, next to my sister's children, who could sit next to my brother's children, who could sit next to her seven grandchildren.

"To be continued," my aunt whispered and ran off to fill several sippy cups with juice.

My cousin Ian, who was always on a diet, asked where John and I had gone for dinner and what John had eaten. "I don't need all the details," he said, fingering a hard-boiled egg on the table, rolling it around in the salty water. "I just want to know. Does he eat carbs?"

My cousin David's wife, Janice, said John looked very sexy when he was interviewing John Ashcroft. Her glasses were attached to a bamboo beaded chain, which hung low around her neck and bounced as she spoke. "He didn't really challenge him," she said. "He seemed to get a little scared at one point when Ashcroft got snippy, but he looked so hot! I mean, it's so cool. How did he even ask you out? Are you having so much fun?"

"He could be with anyone," my cousin Charlie chimed in. "How did you meet?"

"He's not for her," my father said. "He's probably a nice young man, but I don't see them together."

I tried to tell everyone that John and I had only been out twice. I wasn't sure how I felt. Honestly. I liked him, but I didn't think we had that much in common.

"I just hope you don't get hurt," my aunt whispered. "He's so adorable." And then she called out, "Okay, everybody. Let's sit down!"

One of my favorite aphorisms is by the French essayist La Rochefoucauld, who said, "Hypocrisy is the tribute that vice pays to virtue." I mention hypocrisy because it was only after we'd eaten the bitter herbs that I realized how much I liked dating John, not necessarily the man himself, but the idea of dating him. The attention was addictive. It was so refreshing to be able to talk about my social life at one of these family events and not have someone ask if I needed a hug or a tissue. Suddenly I had something fun to offer, and I loved it. That's why I was alternately elated and disgusted with myself when John called that evening to set up our next plan: brunch on Saturday before his flight to Paris.

At brunch, I found out John not only picked up his own dry cleaning on a regular basis—he didn't believe in using personal assistants for that sort of thing—but also preferred a cab to the airport, forgoing the network limousine.

We had French food this time, at a restaurant decorated to look like an art deco bistro—black-and-white tiled columns with smoky mirrors. The place was practically empty, only a few stray diners, as they did most of their brunch business on Sundays.

Our waiter chewed his bottom lip and bounced slightly on the balls of his feet as he recited the specials. I assumed he was an actor, the type who was sent in for roles in Bret Easton Ellis movies like "preppie, world-weary, former coke addict."

"We have a pear-stuffed French toast with citrus marmalade," he said. "And a potato and andrew-y, I mean ann-dooly, I mean andouille sausage—C'mon, Seth, get a grip—omelette served with an artichoke mousse." He took a deep breath, put his hand on his chest, and then rolled his eyes at John, who smiled patiently. "I'm not always like this," the waiter said. "I'm just such a big fan. I mean Sting was in here the other day, and I didn't even flinch, but anyway, I'm going to go get your large sparkling water now." He turned around. "Oh wait, you said flat, didn't you? No, it was sparkling. God, I'm losing it."

Then Seth looked over at me. "Hi," he said, anxiously.

"Hi," I said.

Then he walked away, his head bowed.

"He loves you," I said.

"Well," John said, smiling. "There are all those rumors about me being gay. It comes with the territory if you're a bachelor over thirty-five." He looked at his watch. "I just hope he comes back to take our order. I need to make my plane."

I looked over at the waiter, who was now placing two tall, blue bottles onto a round tray. I wondered if, even for just a moment, he'd imagined himself as John's boyfriend. The matching Prada tuxedos they would wear to the television correspondents dinner in Washington, which was a few weeks away. The photo of them that would appear in *People* magazine and be read at nail salons all over the city. The photo that every single person who teased him in high school would see. Poor, poor Seth the waiter, I thought. That is, until it occurred to me that in the past few days I had wondered myself many, many times what I would wear to the same event. My fantasy was even more disturbing, as it involved complications and debates. Should I wear something slinky off the rack at Yves Saint Laurent or something hip by Chloé or ask Isaac Mizrahi to design one of the beautiful tea-length dresses I had seen him do with a full crinoline underneath? I reached for a piece of bread, but thought twice when I realized that I'd better start dieting soon, as the camera adds ten pounds.

Did I feel so awful about my life that I needed to resort to this sort of public adulation? The kind I had always silently mocked. Was I secretly hoping this public baptism would wash me clean of my ordinariness? Apparently, the answer was: yes. True, John and I always had things to say. I liked him. I did, but I knew there was something else at work. I was always asking myself how much and why? And then it occurred to me: I was in a ménage à trois: It was John, my worst self, and me. The three of us were sitting in that restaurant, waiting for our omelettes to arrive.

As he cut into his eggs, which he said were a little underdone, John discussed his past relationships. He told me he'd had very few, and generally ended things not with a long discussion, something he hated, but with a note.

"How does that usually go over?" I asked.

"Fine," he said. "So far, I only had one woman threaten to cut up the sweater I gave her for Christmas."

A FEW DAYS later at the gym, I ran into a guy who was a writer on my last show. Barry was dark and squat. His gym shorts hugged his hairy thighs, and his tall, yellowing sweat socks came to his knees. I had seen him a few times in the last couple of weeks, never actually exercising, but instead imagining what exercise he would do if he were to exercise. He lingered by the free weights, debating whether to use thirty- or fifty-pound barbells. Then he walked away. He perched at the base of the treadmill, examining the electronic keypad with all the many lights and sounds, deciding whether to walk or run, but he never did, instead going to the stretching mat, where he sat, looking out the window absently.

Barry told me he had sold a few movies. He asked me how I was. I said good. Then I changed it to great. He always asked me about work. Did I miss working in TV? Did I miss the money? In the past, I'd tried to make my dating column sound more exciting than it really was, all the letters I got from all over the country ("from Las Vegas and Florida!"), but today, rather than get into all that, I mentioned that I had gone on a few dates with John.

"I know. You told me," he said.

"I did?" I said.

He patted me gently on the shoulder. "Yeah, a couple of times."

This was bad. I thought envisioning my *Vogue* spread was bad enough, but this was worse.

"I'm going to end it," I told Eve later that night. "Even though there isn't exactly anything to end, I think it's the right thing to do."

"Why?" she said. "You like his company. He's smart."

"His company is fine," I said. "It's mine I'm starting to wonder about."

I told her I was having all sorts of doubts about my motives. She told me just to enjoy it. I told her that was exactly the problem. I was enjoying "it" more than I was enjoying him. This is when relationships, however brief, become a lot like apartments with lead paint: you don't even know you're in one until you realize you need to get out.

"So break up with him," she said. "Who cares. You're not going to marry the guy."

"I have to do it," I said.

"You have to break up. You have to," I told myself. Throughout our next date, which lasted several hours, we went for a walk in Central Park on a gray, moody afternoon. I had studied the *New York Times* carefully in preparation for our date, reading about everything from the chaotic recent elections in

Macedonia to the change in parking regulations on Staten Island. There was a long silence as we passed by the statue of Alice in Wonderland near the boat pond, and so I said, "What do you think about the recent elections in Macedonia?" And he said, "I don't know anything about them." Then we walked for another twenty minutes and I came home.

I hadn't spoken to John for a few days when I received a note in the mail on monogrammed, biscuit-colored stationery. "I think I've met the woman I'm going to marry," it said. "But I wanted to tell you how much I've enjoyed getting to know you." And then, "I hope you find what you're looking for. Hang in there."

"Hang in there?" Eve said when I told her. "What, is he writing poster slogans now? Some pundit he is. What's he going to tell the next girl, 'Keep on Truckin''?"

I told her I had written him a note back, saying that I wished him well.

"You're so fucking polite," she said. "I just hang up the phone and wish them dead." She continued. "Or maimed. Ame, he's a pundit. You went out with him a couple of times. You weren't that into it. Right?" she said. "Right?"

"No, you're right," I said.

When I got off the phone, I got ready for bed. I put on a pair of loose, sea green cotton pajamas, which were stained with drops of coffee and frayed at the edges. I turned on the TV in my small, dark apartment on the Upper West Side. I looked in the mirror, examining my face—the crisp lines I had started to notice around my eyes; the freckling along my lip; the faint beige circles my dermatologist said happily were not dangerous moles but instead "just age spots." It was a face that was anonymous to many, but familiar to me. Sort of.

· 6 ·

QUEEN OF THE COURT

AFTER I LEARNED to ride a bicycle at thirty-five, I decided to take on the list of skills I had always wanted to learn. This list included scuba diving, even though I hadn't been in the ocean in over ten years and could only dog paddle, and painting, my great passion in high school, when I did a series of nude, deeply depressed women lying under tables in the fetal position. I began with tennis.

Because my whole family played tennis, my mother enrolled me in group lessons at an early age, but soon it became clear that I had the hand-eye coordination of someone with the wrong eyeglass prescription. It seemed I was always chosen last when we were dividing into teams, and once I was even picked after a girl on crutches. Every spring, when my family would travel down to Miami, my sister and brother played doubles with my parents, while I attended arts and crafts at the local senior center. I sat in an airless, poorly lit room, painting plaster Indian chief heads with white-haired women named Sidelle and Gussie, who debated the merits of prunes versus bran. My mother tried to convince me that by enrolling me in these classes she was merely encouraging my artistic talent, but I think she was trying to spare me the hard truth that when it came to tennis, I was about as athletic as a plaster Indian chief.

As an adult I considered tennis lessons to be part of what I optimistically referred to as "my pre-midlife crisis," as I expected to have another midlife crisis in my forties. This line of thinking suggested that I hoped to live well into my eighties, and managed to be both fatalistic ("I'll hit a peak of misery every decade") and optimistic ("but at least I'll live to a ripe old age"). I thought about all the fifty-year-old men who start dressing like Goths and get tattoos that say "Hell Raiser," whose midlife dilemmas are a reaction to the confines of career, marriage, and children, but I had none of those, which defined itself as a crisis of its own.

As my father put it, "You're living with a whole lot of borscht right now." This was around the same time he said, "You know, if you want to bring home a woman, I could be okay with that." When I told him I wasn't gay, not even a little, he said, "I know, but I'd just like you to find somebody already.

I've met some nice lesbian couples recently, they're very matronly, but they seem very happy together."

"But I'm not gay," I said.

"Okay," he said, appearing less than convinced. "But I'm just saying if that's something you want to do, I'd accept it."

I had the feeling my father was picturing me with an older, heavyset woman with a buzz cut and thin drizzle of hair that grazed the collar of her Indigo Girls T-shirt, the kind of woman who would drive me to family functions on the back of her hog. When I told a few male friends about my conversation with my father, they said things like "That sounds hot!" and "Way to go, Murray!" Another guy said, "You should have told him the only bush you're going to visit is the African bush." The more I dealt with men who said, "If you go gay, can I watch?" the more I thought maybe my father's suggestion might not be so bad.

EVERYONE SAID TENNIS lessons were a great idea, but I felt a little defensive about such an indulgence. I justified the cost by telling myself that if I had children I would be spending all my money on them: on outfits they would adamantly refuse to wear or summer camps they would remember as traumatic. But since I didn't have children, I could afford to take a few tennis lessons.

I found a teacher named Randy, who wore mirrored wraparound sunglasses and a tight baseball cap over his curly, light brown hair. He wore long, slouchy shorts and a loose T-shirt over his pale skin. Every week he greeted me with "Yo! AC in da' mo' fo' house! What be up?"

After a few lessons alone, he announced that I was ready for a clinic with two other beginners. I didn't pay much attention to Natalie, except to notice that she didn't seem as precious as many of the women I knew who sent their children to private school and summered in the Hamptons. There was something elegantly rough about her, which I liked. Every week she marched her slim body onto the court, announcing with a pointed lack of daintiness, "Today I wanna break a sweat! None of this standing-around wussy crap!"

The other member of our group was Geeta, an Indian woman with a clipped English accent. She was petite, with short, thick black hair encased in a heavy sheen of hair spray, and she always wore fitted separates, creased along the leg. She rarely made eye contact, but when she did, she seemed disgusted by my lumpy sweats. I imagined her thinking America would be a better place if it enforced a rigid caste system.

When Randy explained the vital importance of quick steps in getting to the ball, Geeta leaned over and whispered, "Oh no, I hope he doesn't make us run today!" She adjusted her large, tortoise Chanel sunglasses, sliding them more securely onto the bridge of her nose. "When I signed up for tennis, I didn't think there would be so much running." She rolled her r's as she spoke. "I do so hate to run."

The drill was called "Queen of the Court." You rallied with

Randy until you lost, at which point the next person in line would step in. Geeta and I waited on the side for our turn.

"Give it to me, Slick!" Natalie yelled, running from side to side, whacking the ball so hard it seemed she might pop the strings on her racquet. "Don't be a puss!"

Because Randy told us to stay limber, as our turn would come any minute, I shifted from side to side, trying to keep my muscles agile, while Geeta stood with her arms folded, occasionally glancing at her watch or checking to make sure her manicure had not chipped.

"I have very young sons," she explained. "I am only taking lessons so I can play with them, and they aren't very good. I don't need to make too much of this." She directed her attention to the court. "What's a mother to do, am I right?"

Not knowing quite how to answer her, I mumbled, "Absolutely."

"Tell me again where your children school?" Geeta asked. But before I could answer, she said, "Oh, no! I completely forget every week, don't I? Every week you tell me you have no children. You have no children, and I completely forget." She laughed. "Why do I do that?"

"You must be thinking of Natalie," I said.

"But you are the one with the husband who works at the bank, am I correct?"

"No, actually I'm not married."

She slapped her forehead. "Oh, that's right. You have no children and you're not married! Every week I completely forget that you're not married." She nodded as if she were making a mental note not to make the same mistake the following week. "Well, I think your backhand is improving nicely."

"Geeta, let's move it, c'mon, hustle!" Randy yelled. Geeta then sauntered onto the court, turned to face the net, and stood still with her hands dangling at her sides.

"It's good to get the adrenaline flowing," Natalie said, trying to get her breath. She watched Geeta jump away from the ball as it came to her.

"You have to go toward the ball, Geeta!" Randy called over to her. "Go toward the ball. Yeah, that's right."

"Uch, he's such a good teacher, so patient, even when we're being completely spazzy," Natalie said, admiring the way Randy encouraged Geeta not to cower when the ball came her way. "I so want him to teach my kids. You know? I think he'd be so good with them. Especially my daughter, but the problem is how to get her from school on the East Side over to lessons across town. I work. My nanny has to take care of my son. My daughter gets out at three-fifteen, and I can't rush her too much, because the kid moves like molasses. You know what I mean?"

It was a very reasonable question; I just had no idea how to answer her. She might as well have been asking me how to land a 747. Listening to these women talk about their children made me consider even more the fact that I did not have my own. Now, I was quickly approaching the age where, when I did decide to have children, I might need the kind of fertility drugs that could cause you to bear so many children at once that it seemed appropriate to give birth in a cardboard box under the bed and then lick them clean. And while I could make jokes about the subject, the reality, that I had waited so long and could encounter real problems having children, scared me. Although I seldom heard it discussed, I had noticed in my thirties a certain divide between women who were married with children and their single, childless friends. We cared about one another and were still close, but often without even realizing it, we seemed regularly to make assumptions about one another. Many of my single friends and I discussed the fact that if you went out to dinner with a married friend, the odds were very good she might lean across the table, cock her head, and say sadly into your eyes, "No one you like yet?" giving the distinct impression that she had won the grand prize in life—the washer/dryer, car, and trip to Hawaii—while you had picked the curtain with the pyramid of canned squid. It wasn't even children or marriage that were really the issue, it was the whiff of pity that was so often unmistakable, as if they were uncomfortable about having so much when you had so little. If you said that you were happy, the same woman might squeeze your hand, her voice choking, and say, "You're so strong. I don't know if I could be as strong if I were in your position."

In conversations, single friends often referred to themselves as "we" and new mothers as "them."

"Have you noticed they have these witching hours," my

friend Rachel confessed one day over lunch. "The hours when they're either getting their kids ready for day care or school, or they just got home from ceramics class or swimming or French. My friend's two-year-old is studying French. Or they can't talk because they're trying to get the kids to sleep? It's like the cable company with these mothers. You can only call between noon and three, and then you never know."

Our divide was widened by silence because if we said anything, it was assumed we were jealous. Or bitter. Or both. Or didn't understand how difficult their lives were. And maybe we didn't.

As my friend Eve pointed out, "With your single friends you can talk for hours about how some guy hasn't called you since last night. You can focus on yourself. But if you were ready to stick your head in an oven, it would have to take a backseat to someone's kid falling off the sofa. Any need you have is deemed selfish. Plus with new mothers, if they want to talk about their kids, that's what you talk about. You can't say 'Give me the *Reader's Digest* version of your trip to the playground.' With my single friends, when I need it to be, it can be all about me and my life. But with my friends with kids, I have to be ready to disappear at any moment."

My single friends and I complained that many of our friends with children thought we had nothing but free time, never understanding how difficult it is to organize your life when you always have to keep it flexible. When you are dating, you are often subjected to long and time-consuming phone conversations. Conversations that begin with the words "Hello. I'm your cousin's husband's mother's doctor," or "I do accounting for the man who used to sell handbags in your father's showroom five years ago, but he doesn't know me very well." Wanting to be a good sport, you talk to the person for anywhere from ten minutes to an hour. Listening as they say things like "All I know about you is you've got all your limbs and you're not deformed. Right?" or "You wear a heart monitor to work out? Let me ask you a question. Do you ever wear your heart monitor when you're having sex?" You agree to meet this person at a bar or restaurant, for the next forty-five minutes to three-plus hours. You are entirely alone. You smile politely as they say, "You didn't know pornos were available on DVD? Where have you been? I have hundreds!" or "My last girlfriend and I broke up less than a month ago. She said if she finds me with anyone, she'll kill me." He drinks some wine. "And her." After that you drink your wine quickly, eyeing the bottle in case you'll need it for self-defense.

It wasn't that I had so much free time; it was just that unlike my married friends with children I had very little to show for it. In fact, if I added up all the time I spent setting up the first date, choosing what to wear, meeting for drinks or dinner or coffee or brunch, coming home not sure I was into him, but wanting him to call anyway, getting the call, anticipating the second date, choosing what to wear again, going on the second date, deciding I kind of liked him, going on a third date, deciding I really liked him, going out a few more times, fantasizing about our bike trip to Italy, getting more serious, feeling happy to be alive, wondering if things were getting weird or whether it was just my imagination, obsessing over why things didn't work out, chastising myself for not trusting my instincts in the first place, losing a week or four to mild then extreme depression, slowly feeling better, vowing to forge ahead and not get jaded, starting the whole process all over again, I could have gotten my M.D. Read all of Proust. And written an opera. In German. Twice. That's what I wanted to say when these women asked me what it was like to have so much free time.

AFTER MY TENNIS lesson, my habit was to phone my sister, Holly, on my cab ride home, hoping to catch her when she had a few free minutes between running her decorating business and shuttling her children from school to whatever after-school activity they had scheduled for that day. This afternoon I managed to get her as she was stopping at the bagel place, a little something for her son to snack on before soccer practice.

"So," she inquired eagerly. "Tell me about the date last night. How was the urologist? Did you like him?"

Like many well-intentioned people, a woman I knew from the gym had fixed me up based on the popular "He's single, you're single, you never know" approach. This is when being unmarried feels an awful lot like being in a bad science fiction film, where people in hooded polyester bodysuits, stripped of any specificity or identity, mill about in a dreary moon colony and are mated with each other as "Woman X5419 meet Man G6543. Proceed." It was this kind of random logic that made me want to suggest a possible friendship for them based on the always solid "You're married. They're married. You'll have lots in common!" I tried to explain that even women they perceived as desperate, even women of a "certain age," had standards. I wanted to explain too that often because we'd waited so long to meet the right person and had learned to live on our own, we were more discriminating, not less.

The urologist was a nice, if slightly wooden fellow, who talked in great detail about how he liked to install sophisticated stereo equipment in his home entertainment system so as to actually feel his video game sound effects. He was a little stiff when he asked, "May I inquire as to whether you have any hobbies?"

"Mmm," I said, smiling. "Worrying about the rest of my life?"

He frowned.

"I don't understand," he said. "I meant do you like music or art? For example, I like Kenny G and impressionist paintings. Were you making a joke?"

"He was fine," I now told my sister. "Just not for me."

"How do you know?" she pressed. "It was only one date. I'm just asking, really, because I'm genuinely interested," she said, as if we were discussing not my social life, but a subject to which the Learning Channel might devote an hour, like the mating rituals of penguins. "You're the one who always says how nervous you are on the first date, and now you're saying you don't like someone. But how do you know he's not nervous too?"

When I did go out with someone who said things like "How's about we chow in the P.M.?" or another guy who said he had never dated a woman who hadn't been hospitalized for depression at least once, usually because of him, the problems were obvious; but it was in these more subtle situations, where I couldn't say there was anything actually wrong with the guy except that he wasn't for me, that I was pressed to defend my decision. I thought about Eve, who said that her family pushed her to give every date a second chance. "I realized the only way to get my family off my back was to say that a man was a drug addict. That worked for a while, but now they're saying, 'Maybe you can help him quit.' "

Even though my sister had dated a bit before she met her husband fifteen years ago, as I would describe a date to her I would feel that I was describing nothing short of life in a foreign land, and I could just as easily have been describing not my date with a urologist, but whether to cook goat or monkey before my tribe went on a hunt.

"How do you know after one date?" she said.

"You just know."

"How?"

"I wasn't attracted to him."

My father often asked me whether or not I thought attraction grew. With him, I found an answer that worked. "Maybe,"

I would say. "Maybe I would think that someone I initially found completely unattractive was more attractive than I first thought, but I would never feel hot for him. I would never have sex with him, and there would be no grandchildren. Ever." That kept him quiet.

For the purposes of our conversation, my answer worked. But what I liked most about physical attraction was that unlike other, more abstract qualities, it was as close to an absolute truth as you could get. You either were attracted or you weren't. Otherwise you could drive yourself crazy with questions like: How do you know if he's the one? Is the concept of "the one" naive? Can you ever really know? Am I settling? Have I given up hope without realizing it? Should I have given someone along the way another chance? Will I ever feel that I know anything at all, and if not, what then?

My sister continued. "Laura Lautenstein wasn't attracted to her husband at all on the first date or the second date and look at them now. They're incredibly happy."

I had been hearing about these couples—the ones who didn't like each other at first only to fall madly in love—for what seemed like forever.

"Are you telling me you think I should go out with the urologist again?"

"I'm just saying how can you know from only one date?" she said. "You never know."

It was always my sneaking suspicion that when people said "You never know," they were really saying, "*You* never know—yourself, you—because if you had better judgment, you'd be married like me."

"You do know," I huffed, handing the cabdriver a few wilted bills. "I'm home. I have to go."

I planned to point out to her later that people who allow themselves to be fixed up actually want to meet someone and are therefore the ones most likely to give a date the fairest shot every step of the way. I also wanted to point out that if you go out with someone twice, why not go out fifty times? Why not take a road trip to the Berkshires? You might deeply hate the person by then, but at least you'd get to see Tanglewood. And while we're at it, if you're asking how we know if we like another person, why not go for broke and ask how we know if we like anything? How do you know you like Irving Penn's photographs? Japanese food? That you're not on fire right now? That you're even real? How do you know anything at all?

When I arrived in the lobby of my apartment building, the attendant, a lovely round man named Jorge, called over to me.

"Emma," he called. "This." He handed me a portly envelope. "Here this got you."

The envelope contained my new lease, one that offered the option to stay in the building for one or two more years. Now, for some, this might have been cause for celebration, as my one-bedroom apartment was roomy and inexpensive for Manhattan. Many of my neighbors had lived in their apartments for over forty years, and when, as was often the case, our water was shut off for a few days or the elevators broke down, people took to scrawling Socialist graffiti in the mailbox area in the lobby, writing in shaky ballpoint pen on the notices themselves, "You can't treat the people like this! We will rise up!" It seemed my building was full of Stanley Kowalskis who, when it was announced that a large air-conditioning pipe would be fitted into the back of the building, connected to a new restaurant below, wrote, "I've got a friend, a powerful friend at City Hall who's gonna hear about this!" Other tenants suggested that holiday decorations be banned in the lobby as the division between church and state should be upheld even in small communities. Holding the envelope between my fingers made me remember the last time I'd held a lease, and how I wondered then whether I should sign on for one or two more years because that was such a long time and I was so sure I was going to meet someone and eventually move in with him that maybe I should choose to pay month to month. And now two years later I wasn't even close.

I'd mentioned this to Eve, who told me that not wanting to renew her lease, a decision she faced every year, actually thrilled her (she was also the same person who once said she felt as if she had "nosebleed seats to her own life"), because it suggested she was more optimistic about her future than she realized. "It's when I'm ready to buy my own one bedroom that I worry," she explained. "Which, by the way, I am now."

What appeared as infinite freedom one minute—I could go to India for three months, I could go to a movie without having to find a babysitter, I could try a new career without worrying about mortgages or back-to-school shoes—could seem like limbo the next. As I contemplated the white envelope, the word "URGENT," which was scrawled on the back in feathery ink, took on new meaning. At thirty-five, I did not have one thing cementing me to any place or world, and suddenly my life seemed defined not by what I knew, but by all the questions that remained unanswered each and every minute, and then I remembered someone telling me, "All you can ever really count on is yourself in this life." I felt as if my life hadn't quite started, and I was already running late. And then, as I thought more about this, rather than playing Billie Holiday and hiding all the knives, I took a nap.

THE FOLLOWING WEEK, it was my turn to start the round robin as Geeta and Natalie chatted briskly, their heads cocked toward each other. Randy had taught us a list of phrases to help us visualize how we could improve our game. "Gun in the holster!" meant you should keep your racquet at your hip until you were ready to swing. "Sit in the chair!" was a way to keep your body still until the ball came.

"Picture the ice cream cone!" Randy yelled now, as I attempted to serve. This meant I was supposed to hold the ball on the tips of my fingers, toss it, and watch it rise into the air until it hit my racquet strings. "You're not seeing it, AC! Imagine the ice cream flavor, see the chocolate chip or the rum raisin and whatever."

As I came off the court, I heard Geeta say, "And now I've lost my weekend nanny who sleeps over both nights, and they are simply impossible to find. We offered her twice as much per night, but she refused." She rolled her eyes. "She claims she's pregnant."

Natalie shook her head.

"We're so lucky," Natalie said. "Our nanny is like family. When there was that anthrax scare, we stockpiled antibiotics for her too. And when my little Max had a cold, she sat by his side."

"Natalie you're up!" Randy yelled.

As I walked off the court, Geeta, her arm outstretched, waved by moving all of her fingers rapidly at once. "This week I remembered you're not married!" she called over.

"Still not married!" I answered.

And then we had nothing to say. In that moment, I was sure if I'd had children or a husband we could have made the kind of dull chitchat I would complain about later. I had tried to talk with her about restaurants once, but when I did, she twirled the short strands of hair above her ears, looking away and saying only, "My husband and I have never been there. You go there with your friends, do you?"

Standing there in silence, I said something that I would recall a few hours later with a certain amount of shame. "I used to be a television writer," I announced, my delivery infused with a quality of desperation. "For four years. I was a producer too." I rolled my eyes and nodded my head. "We worked such crazy hours. Crazy." In mentioning this fact, I was trying simultaneously to explain why I wasn't married and also to convince her that I too had a vital, exciting life. I think I was actually trying to convince myself.

Geeta held on to both of her elbows, her arms crossed. "Oh really," she said, managing a perplexed grin. "I'm sorry, I don't watch television. But my three children enjoy it and so does my husband."

Later in the hour, Randy remarked that he had never seen me hit the ball quite so hard.

Unlike the week before, Geeta was now running toward the ball with so much fervor that she ran past it. Once she even ran into the fence. I stood silently with Natalie. On her hand, now gripping her racquet, a big, fat diamond glimmered. I studied her, imagining her daily life as completely different from mine. I imagined she took her children, who had crisp blue eyes, to school every morning at the same time. While I could eat a dinner of leftover salad, a few spoonfuls of peanut butter, an orange, some turkey bologna, a handful of tortilla chips, and for dessert, a couple of sticks of gum, Natalie, I was sure, shopped for well-rounded meals, proteins and starches to be served alongside leafy greens, which had been proven in a few studies in Holland to reduce the risk of both colon cancer and juvenile diabetes. As she helped her children with their homework, I talked on the phone with my friends about such subjects as "learning to live with ambivalence," and how to distinguish between a man with a strong feminine side and one who couldn't admit he was gay.

"That's okay, Geeta! Good try!" Natalie yelled, clapping loudly. She turned to me as if she wanted to say something but couldn't, and I assumed that she was trying to make conversation because it was the polite thing to do, but really there was nothing unifying us.

"Wow, that Geeta really stinks, doesn't she?" she said, under her breath. "I mean, she's a nice lady, but she can't hit a ball to save her goddamned life. We're so much better. We've gotta get her the hell outta here and fast."

Since I had been thinking the same thing for the last three weeks, I was surprised to hear Natalie say it first. "I mean, I have a lot of expenses in my life and these lessons are my one goddamn luxury," she continued, watching as Geeta went running with her racquet perched high above her head, yelling, "Oh dear! Oh dear!" as the ball landed in the center of the adjoining court, where two older, very serious players proceeded to glare at her.

"Do you think we can?" I asked.

"I'm gonna see what I can do," she said. "But I think we can get rid of her. She told me she thinks she's gotten enough already, and God knows I've gotten enough of her. Hey, do you need a lift home? I've got my car today."

Forty-five minutes later, I was strapped into the front seat of Natalie's large, caramel Suburban, the telltale signs of children—empty juice boxes and erasable markers—all over the pile rug.

"I'm sorry the car's such a shithole," she said, throwing several pop-up books into the backseat. "We take this car back and forth to our country house, and with kids there's no way to keep anything clean. Plus, the boxers rub their asses against everything. They're sweet dogs, but they smell like ass."

She looked in the rearview mirror, running her fingers through her long, light brown hair. "You know, I want to get better highlights since the gray is coming in, but I don't have time, you know?"

I was reminded of a conversation I'd had recently with my father.

"Look what I see," he said, smiling. "Someone's got their first gray hair."

I made a quick dash for the bathroom nearby. "Where are the tweezers?"

My father followed me.

"Sweetheart, I'm sorry I said anything because now it seems like you're getting all worked up about this," he said. "You're beautiful." He pointed to a small patch of gray at his temple. "Besides, it's not a bad thing. I've got them too."

"But you're seventy-four years old!" I said.

Natalie continued to examine her hair.

"My colorist's on crack," she said. "Look at all this gray!"

"Oh yeah," I said, hoping to unite us, as we were the same age. "I'm getting so much gray I feel like Indira Gandhi." But then there was silence. It seemed further proof we had nothing in common. But then something changed.

"So what's it like?" she said, staring straight ahead. "Y'know, being you. Is it great? It must be great. Randy said you wrote for TV. What famous people have you met? Have you seen any of them naked? You've got so much freedom. By the way, don't get me wrong, I love my life. I love my husband, my kids; I wouldn't give them up for the world, but just for a week I'd love to have your life."

I was even less prepared for her next comment.

"C'mon, lemme live vicariously through you for the next twenty blocks. Tell me about all the wild things you do. The restaurants. The clubs. The parties. The men. God, there must be so many of them. It must be so exciting to meet someone new and have that thrill when you go to bed with them for the first time. That rush of new bodies and all the lust. Let me tell you, you only have that thrill once." She twisted her wedding ring. "You have other nice things, but never that."

I thought of how disappointed she'd be if I told her I often got into my pajamas by six. Or my most recent blind date, who asked me to meet him in Central Park at nine-thirty at night. When he asked how he'd know who I was, I said, "I'll be the one with the rape whistle around her neck."

"You don't want to hear about my life," I said.

"Yes I do! Oh, God, yeah I really do!" she said, her voice betraying something deeper and more urgent. "Tell me all about your life. Please. And start with something juicy."

I realized just how much I had been assuming that if I had her life, I would be asking so many fewer questions about mine, and how maybe that was the biggest misconception of all. And then I thought about how the real question wasn't when I would meet someone or have children, but why I would think that having them would be the answer to so many things, everything really. That question bore more questions. What did that say about me? Wasn't that a recipe for disaster? Did I rely on that fantasy to help me through my reality? Did I really think those things were going to make everything better? And suddenly, I missed all my old questions, which now seemed simple by comparison.

"Yeah, and add lots of details," she said, her voice rising with excitement. "Tell me more about all the men. I wanna see the whole thing clearly."

· 7 ·

MY SAMSONITE

Recently I went to dinner with a man who, after our first date, was committed to a mental hospital. At least that's what I decided today was the reason he hadn't called. And although I knew this wasn't true, I still thought: "Maybe I'll go visit him."

Martin had a mopey charm and the haunted quality of someone who regularly imagined his life flashing before his eyes, the kind of man who could glimpse a plastic butter knife lying on a picnic table and envision it impaling his jugular. He kissed me within ten minutes of meeting me and then said, "Was that weird? Was that too fast? No, right? Good."

We went for Italian food at a restaurant known for its inspired pizzas. He ordered a salad for dinner, explaining that he was between trainers and acting jobs. Martin, with his short, blond ringlets and green eyes, looked like a grown-up version of the kind of cherub often depicted on bronzed lawn ornaments. It wasn't hard to imagine him perched on a birdbath giggling with a jug over his head.

Over antipasto, he confided, "I suffer from occasionally crippling depression. My mother was inattentive." I had a fleeting thought my love could save him. He kissed me again. But now, two weeks later, I hadn't heard from him.

I read that among members of the Hmong people in Thailand, when a man is interested in a woman, he approaches her and tugs at a piece of string at her waist. They then wander off together for a chat, and if this goes well, he ultimately "kidnaps" the girl from her parents' house. You have to admit, it's a bold way of saying you care. What I also like about this scenario is that instead of waiting for a phone call, as I was now, I would be the one placing it from an undisclosed location. "I know you haven't heard from me in a while, but the good news is I have a boyfriend!"

I was not getting anything done today. I was supposed to be working, writing a column for a weekly paper about whether love is a choice or a force. Is love all in the timing? Do people choose to fall in love when it fits into their lives? Or is it a force, dictated by fate or the stars? I grew up thinking love was like a lightning bolt. My father said that when he met my mother, he was powerless. "I looked at her and I just knew, but she was dating my friend, Sol, so I asked him if I could take her out and he said, 'If you can feed her, you can have her.'" But now I found myself wondering how exactly love ever happens. Martin and I had a good date. A good date should mean something. A good date should matter. It doesn't have to mean everything, but it should matter for something.

I'd heard people list what matters to them, everything from sense of humor to physical fitness to "should be spiritual but not necessarily religious." Would this person be a good parent? Is he wild in bed? Must like Nirvana and Django Reinhardt. Must be crazy for simple pleasures like Scrabble and big dogs. Must be sensitive, but not soft. Feisty, but not bitchy. But even when they found all those things in a person, it didn't seem to matter enough. And then I found myself asking again: What actually matters? When the billionaire J. Paul Getty was asked, "How much money is enough?" he answered, "Just a little bit more." Is that the problem? That people think they know what they want, but when they find it, they realize they actually want just a little bit more? In my last relationship, I wanted to get married, and he wanted to live together indefinitely and ultimately that's what broke us up. He wanted a little bit more time. I wanted a little bit more of a commitment. Now I just wanted Martin to call so I could say, "Don't ever call me again."

Instead, I called my friend Phoebe.

I asked if she wanted to see *Spellbound*, a documentary about the 1999 National Spelling Bee Championship. She said yes. When I got to the theater, the line was already snaking around the block. A stray piece of loose-leaf paper was taped over the box office window and said "Seven o'clock sold out." It was warm, the slow, hazy end to a sticky day. I looked at the girls spilling onto the sidewalk, standing on either side of the subway grating so as to avoid their high heels falling through. Is that what men want? Do they want a Japanese girl who, in the middle of summer, sports leg warmers and the kind of cutoff gloves Fagin wore in *Oliver*? The chunky punk with soft thighs and a heart of gold? Or maybe one of those cool blondes who uses the word "lovely" all the time instead of admitting her utter contempt for everything? The kind of woman who says after a date, "He was lovely, just lovely, but he wasn't for me," which really means "He was disgusting, and I wouldn't be caught dead with him, but he liked me so I'll try to be kind." Because if that's what men want, I was in trouble.

Actually, I'd been thinking I was in trouble anyway. Maybe I was too sarcastic. Maybe I scared people. When someone asked if I spoke any other languages, like French or Spanish, I often answered, "No, but I speak the language of paranoia and insecurity fluently." Maybe I needed to stop doing that. Or maybe it was my thighs. I'd joked on occasion that I had a hot body for a grandmother of six. Maybe I had to stop doing that too. I needed to be more confident. My confidence waned because of things like Martin not calling me after our date when he specifically said, "I'll call you." Why didn't he call? Maybe he wanted someone who did yoga and told him he had a beautiful practice. Maybe he wanted someone to stroke him while he was in a fetal position, crying for the mother he never had.

Or maybe he wanted someone like the cool blonde who would throw eerily perfect dinner parties and arrange her closet alphabetically, according to designer. Or the Japanese girl in the leg warmers, who radiated possibilities. She seemed so comfortable with her body. I, on the other hand, was not. When I was growing up, in our house nudity was defined as the period of time between the shower and your towel. And while I don't consider myself prudish, I'm not one of those girls who is up for anything. I once dated a man who told me he liked to have sex with cakes. "With cakes?" I said. "Yeah," he said. "You smash the cake with your bodies, smear it all over each other and then lick it off." When he told me this, I remember thinking: "Talk about yeast infections." The Japanese girl looked like a cake girl. She would say, "Cakes! Yeah! That's totally hot!" Unlike me, who said, "Do you put down a tarp?"

I watched the couples on line. A man and woman slouched in matching white tank tops. They were equally pierced and tattooed, with colorful sleeves of ink that covered their arms completely. Is that what they bonded over? Did they say, "Tonight, let's go get a dragon on my ass!" and "Honey, should I pierce my other nipple?" The two men ahead of me held hands, united, it seemed, by their love of tight, white T-shirts and steroids. A slender girl with a ponytail and a preppy, green wraparound skirt nuzzled the deltoid of the much older man she was with. After years of therapy, she'd come to terms with her Daddy complex. What did these people know that I didn't?

Phoebe got out of a cab. She was tall with dark, close-set eyes and short, blond hair. She had long, shapely legs—the kind that would look perfect sticking out of a tap-dancing cigarette box—and usually carried a big, brown saddlebag dangling at her hip, filled with books. This time it was *The Sun Also Rises*. She also had three different types of mints of varying strengths and even occasionally something like a vintage postcard with a photograph of nineteenth-century sunbathers in long sleeves and knickers, which she picked up at a flea market three years ago.

"Shit," she said, looking at the long line. "Who invited them?"

"I know, it's like a Stones concert. Should we get tickets for the ten o'clock?"

Phoebe explained that she'd forgotten she had dinner plans. I decided to go to the ten o'clock anyway, alone, and Phoebe offered to keep me company while I ate dinner before. I suggested one of my favorite restaurants, Blue Ribbon Bakery, which was only a few blocks away. Josh and I used to go there all the time. For the two years after we broke up, I avoided it since I was always afraid I'd run into him with his girlfriend, but in the last year, I'd started coming again. It seemed somehow appropriate that given the anxiety I associated with this restaurant, it specialized in comfort foods: thick, pillowy slices of bread; deli meats layered in tight circles; a well-researched matzoh ball, honed to be both lumpy and light, swimming in salty broth.

Blue Ribbon Bakery was on the corner of Downing and Bedford streets, housed in a large room encased by tall glass windows so that each table had a view of the high drama that was occasionally the foot traffic outside. Late on Saturday night it was not uncommon to sit by the window and see glamorous, bony couples stumbling home, ones who would ask each other's name in the morning. Or a harried man rushing by in tights and tiara. Once in a while too you'd see a pair in love, moving quietly and confidently forward, toward home, breaking your heart because they were so damned happy. The kind that made you think, "When did I get so bitter?"

It was not uncommon to wait an hour to be seated, but tonight we were not only given a table immediately, but the best one in the house, against the window so as to have the clearest view of the street, with a wide ledge to rest our bags.

"Can I get you ladies an alcoholic beverage on this lovely evening?" our waitress said.

"Wine," Phoebe and I requested in unison.

"The Bianchetta if you have it," Phoebe added.

Our waitress was stout, with a fleshy, sweet smile into which her eyes receded. Her hair was several reds and oranges, as if she'd asked her colorist to create every shade of a raging inferno. She had jagged bangs, an inch long at most, that looked as if she cut them with plastic children's scissors. The bangs sat above her face like a curtain perched above a stage and were especially dramatic when she arched one of her slender, painted eyebrows.

"The Bianchetta," she said, her Irish accent becoming more noticeable as she pronounced every "ah" sound as an "eh." "Just lovely. A fine, fine choice."

Phoebe excused herself to go to the bathroom downstairs, descending the staircase in the left corner of the room. I watched her as she went. It was now a beautiful night, cooler and breezier than even an hour ago. I was looking toward the staircase, waiting for Phoebe to return, when I saw a man walking downstairs. I could make out only the back of his head, his dark hair short, but not shaved, his narrow shoulders covered by a black jacket. When Phoebe finally returned to the table, I grabbed her arm. "I think I just saw Josh go downstairs," I said. "I only saw him from behind, but I know it was him. Shit."

"Just take a deep breath," she said, and reached for my hand.

I found myself doused in memories of him. I saw Josh the night we met, negotiating his way over to me through the thick crowd of people. At my mother's funeral in his trim Jil Sander suit. Then I remembered one of our last conversations, the one that took place on the phone only a few months after we broke up.

"I need my big suitcase," I said. "I'm going to Cuba with a group and we're taking medicine and clothes down with us to give away, and I need my big suitcase."

"That's cool," Josh said. "You can pick it up whenever you want."

As we spoke, I pictured his small brown eyes, thinning, close-cropped hair, and modestly rebellious sideburns. I wanted to remind him that this was the same big, brown suitcase I had taken on our trip to Paris; the same suitcase from our trip to Spain, where we went to the Guggenheim Bilbao and Josh threw up behind a fifty-foot puppy made of flowers. That night I searched this very suitcase for Pepto-Bismol. We had taken this big suitcase on all our trips together, and now I was taking it to Cuba alone. Well, not exactly alone. A few days earlier, I'd called the company that was organizing my trip and learned some unsettling news. "All I can tell you about your group is there are twenty-two people signed up," the woman on the phone told me. "And the average age is sixty-eight."

Josh told me all about how work had never been better, although the film business was so fickle that he always felt as if he were getting an ulcer. As he continued I thought: "Maybe we can meet for dinner." I missed him.

"I've been seeing someone for a few months now," he said.

Now I was the one ready to throw up behind the giant puppy. A few months? We'd only been broken up a few months.

He had a new girlfriend, and I was going to Cuba with a group of senior citizens. I was just glad I hadn't mentioned all the jokes my friends made. "Does the Copacabana have an early bird special?" And "You might want to bring some Viagra in case you get lucky!"

After Josh and I got off the phone, I remembered that old Samsonite luggage commercial, where the gorilla jumps up and down on a suitcase, slamming it around an empty cage to prove its durability. That suitcase, the commercial suggested, could hold even your heaviest baggage and remain indestructible. Thinking back over our year and a half together, with all the shit Josh and I went through, all the times we could have walked away but didn't, I just kept wishing: "If only our relationship could have been a Samsonite."

Phoebe was calm now, her voice steady. She knew I'd been nervous about coming to this restaurant for a long time. "I bet you a million dollars it's not Josh," she assured me. "The back of his head could be anyone. Look around. Every guy in this restaurant could be Bruce Willis from behind."

She had a point.

"You're so right," I said.

The waitress brought our wine. I took a gulp. And then another. A few more drinks and I'd be Liza Minnelli.

"Thirsty?" the waitress said, winking.

I smiled back, and as I did, I saw the broad, grinning figure that was Fred Feldman, one of Josh's best friends, heading downstairs. We used to go to dinner with him at this very restaurant all the time. "Shit," I said, looking to my left, at the street outside, where Josh's other best friend, Alan, was getting out of a taxi with his girlfriend, Janine. She was wearing a short, lavender cocktail dress with wispy straps. Six months ago, Alan was the one who told me Josh got engaged. We were bicycling around Central Park, and I was on my new skinny, Italian road bike. I was still feeling a huge sense of accomplishment at simply making it around the park with limbs intact, and when Alan told me the news, I kept pedaling and said, casually, "That's so great he's getting married. Tell Josh I'm really happy for him." Then I swerved and hit a hot dog stand.

"Oh my God," I asked the waitress, "is there an engagement party downstairs?"

"Ah, no," she said, and for a moment I was somewhat relieved. "It's not an engagement party. It's a . . ." She snapped her finger. "Oh, how do you say it? The American phrase, I mean. It's eh, eh, eh . . ."

As I waited for her to finish her sentence, I leaned forward in my chair, rocking, jiggling my leg, looking to all the world as if my methadone were wearing off.

She continued. "It's eh, eh . . ." She finally remembered the word. "It's a rehearsal dinner!"

"I'll have another glass of wine, please," I said. "That's my ex-boyfriend downstairs. He's marrying the girl he started dating right after we broke up."

"I'll get your wine," she said and rushed off.

"Bring the bottle," I called after her.

I looked up and saw the man who'd introduced me to Josh. Mark had been living in Los Angeles for the last few years, pursuing a successful career as a music producer whose specialty was breathing new life into big-hair heavy metal bands that were popular in the eighties. He was very tall, and his clothes, crisp and just so, reflected someone who loved Cartier-Bresson photographs and brushed metal furniture. I rushed up to the middle of the dining room, where Mark was standing. I was planning to say, "Mark! It's so great to see you!" but what came out was "Mark! Mark! Is this Josh's rehearsal dinner?"

He put his arm around me, gently. "Ame!" he said. He introduced a woman behind him, who looked like she could have modeled Hawaiian suntan lotion. "No, it's my rehearsal dinner. This is my fiancée, Lara."

I smiled at Lara, who smiled back. I didn't even know he had a girlfriend. "Congratulations," I said.

Mark leaned in and whispered in my ear.

"Josh got married last weekend."

The busboy arrived and seemed confused as to why my eyes got teary when he said, "Who's having the market salad?" I asked him for extra dressing, but what I really wanted to know was: "Can you explain the world to me? Because I don't understand it. How can you be in love one minute, thinking of all the places you'll take your big suitcase for the rest of your lives, and the next minute watch him marry someone else?" I wanted an explanation. I looked around. The summer was swarming with couples and all I could wonder was, "What did Josh and I lack?"

I'd told myself for a few years now that there was a reason I wasn't in love yet. I needed to experience true independence before sharing my life. Maybe I needed to learn to choose better people, as I sometimes joked that my taste in men ranked with Eva Braun's. Maybe there was some lesson I was meant to learn, and I still hadn't gotten it, so I'd be presented with it again and again until I did. I told myself these things in order to feel like there was some order in the universe. Maybe there was a plan for me. The first busboy must have sensed that I wanted to discuss the meaning of life because a different busboy returned with my salad dressing.

"Ame," Phoebe said, leaning across the table.

"Do I look okay?" I asked, pulling down my sleeveless blue T-shirt, which was gathered along one side. When I feel extremely anxious, it often helps me to find a role model. While I knew many solid souls were guided by thinking, "What would Jesus do?" I often thought, "What would Jackie O wear?"

Phoebe said, "You look fantastic."

"I don't look like I'm about to cry?"

"No."

"Just don't let me drink any more wine."

Phoebe had started to say something else when I saw a man's hip, dressed in tailored pants, come into my line of vision. "Hey, look, it's Josh," I said. "Hey Josh." I drank some more wine. I introduced Phoebe, who said hello as she announced she was going to have a smoke outside. Josh took her chair. The one we'd thought was the best seat in the house fifteen minutes ago.

"Hey, Ame," he said, kissing my cheek. "How have you been?"

And then I said what so many ex-girlfriends say when they didn't want it to end. "I've been really, really good," I said. "Sorta great, actually. Really, really great. Hey, I heard you got married. Congratulations."

In the time Josh and I were together, we discussed our wedding a couple of times. These conversations were always hazy and hypothetical, infused with as much joy as a trip to the emergency room. Should we go to a justice of the peace and then have a big party at a loft? What about in his parents' backyard? His mother had just redone the garden, and we could put a gate around the pool so no one would fall in. He was adamant that there be no band. He had played guitar in a wedding band and swore that the only thing wedding musicians hated more than an empty stomach was brides. "We'll have a deejay," he insisted.

"Yeah, it was a nice wedding," he said now. "It was last weekend in Atlanta. Tessa's family is from there. It was a nice wedding. Small. You would have liked it."

My first thought was "I would have liked it to be me." I wished I were sitting there telling Josh about my wedding—the stone barn in Putnam County; the photos of me jumping on a trampoline in my wedding dress; the make-your-own pizzas. The funny, beautiful toast that my father gave that made us all cry. Or at the very least that right now I was going home to my own happy relationship and my own sweet boyfriend, who, upon hearing my story, would take me in his arms and say, "Come here. You had a rough night."

But none of those things was a reality, and so I said, "I'm happy for you, Josh. Congratulations." I felt as if I might cry, but I didn't. And to think, the only reason I was here was to distract myself from Martin not calling. Well, that certainly worked.

"So what's happening with you?" he said.

"I'm really good," I answered. "I'm much more athletic now than when we were together. The other day this trainer at the gym asked me if I wanted to be in his triathlon training course. And I was like 'Me?' And I was flattered, because he actually handpicks the people he wants. So I'm thinking about it."

"Just stop talking," I told myself. "You can do it."

"But I've changed the way I see my life," I continued. My hands were gesturing so dramatically I might as well have been Marcel Marceau. "For some reason, I was so influenced when I read Paul Bowles's obituary. He wrote *The Sheltering Sky,* obviously, but also music, and he was an artist and he lived in Tangier. I just feel like if you can swing it, why not try lots of different careers and live different places? Oh, and I learned to ride a bike. I bought a bike a few months ago. It's Italian."

When I was a small child, my mother told me that because she had me at forty-one, I was considered a high-risk pregnancy and her obstetrician told her I might be born with brain damage. Now, as I continued to go on and on about the trainer, Paul Bowles, and my new bike, I wondered if, in fact, I was.

"Really?" he said. "Well, hey, okay. That's cool." He looked at me, and I knew what he was going to say. "I better get back downstairs. My wife is waiting."

Wife. How fitting, I thought, that the middle word in "wife" was "if." What if I hadn't pushed Josh to get married? What if I hadn't lost my job and my mother hadn't died and we hadn't had so many strains on our relationship? What if I'd met him earlier? Or later? I wondered if we'd still be together. I wondered if I should have been more patient. I wondered if tomorrow my therapist could fit me in.

Phoebe got back from her cigarette, and we got the check.

Putting my face in my hands, I said, "I just don't get it."

"Baby, it doesn't make sense," she said. "Listen, I don't want to leave you, but Claudia has been at that bar waiting for me, and I can't get in touch with her."

"No, I want to go. Let's leave before they tell me they're pregnant," I said. "But first, I just want to go downstairs and say congratulations to Mark and his girlfriend. I was so unhinged when he got here."

"Are you sure you want to do that?" she asked. "You don't have to do that, you know."

"I know," I said, taking a deep breath. "But I've known Mark for years. I've known him through lots of different girlfriends, and we were friends, and I'm happy that he finally found the one. Dammit, I'm happy for everyone! Happy, happy, happy!"

As I got up from the table, I remembered an acting class I took. The teacher, a woman in her seventies with patchy blond hair and chalky skin, told us she had once been considered one of Hollywood's top ingenues and had worked opposite Olivier and Kirk Douglas. She began the class by asking, "Who's ever considered suicide? Anyone? Anyone ever sit in a bath and imagine the blood pouring out of their veins into the warm water? I have." According to her method, everything came down to intention, she said. If you have a clear intention, it doesn't matter what you actually say in a scene because the words become vehicles for the feelings behind them. "For example," she said, "I'm doing a scene where I'm buying a muffin. A dull actor would make it just a boring exchange of bills. 'Thank you for my bran muffin. It's moist.' But let's say my intention in buying the muffin is 'to convince myself that life is worth living,' then I would hand the dollar bill to the cashier differently. The line 'I have exact change' becomes a way to keep yourself alive! 'I have exact change. Exact change!' " Her voice cracked as she choked back tears. She composed herself quickly, as only seasoned actors can.

I realized I was going to need my acting skills when I got downstairs. My heart was beating so fast it felt as if there was a mosh pit in my chest. My intention was a simple one: to say congratulations with a happy, yet dignified tone, then get out as quickly as possible. Actually, my intention should have been to retain my dignity, turn around, and run out of this restaurant immediately, but I didn't. Instead, I walked slowly into the dark basement, convinced that if there was one night I was destined to break my neck and end up at an assisted living facility off the New Jersey Turnpike, this was it.

There were several tables, each in possession of a delicate, flickering candle and a crisp bouquet arranged in a short vase, as this was, after all, a rehearsal dinner. I made my way to Mark's table. He lifted his fork to his mouth and bit some kind of fatty smoked fish.

"Congratulations," I said.

He swallowed. "Ame!" he said. This was impetuous. This was a bad idea. I didn't think this through. What was I thinking? I was too rash sometimes. I'd have to work on that.

Mark's fiancée was in the middle of talking to the person next to her. He tapped her shoulder. She turned around and smiled.

"Well, that's all I wanted to say," I said.

He kissed me and said he'd call me, and I turned around to leave. In the corner, I saw Josh with his new wife, whose head was resting on his shoulder. She was dark-haired with lush blue eyes. She had big breasts, which made mine feel tiny by comparison, as if her breasts were a pair of St. Bernards and mine were Yorkies. I knew every person at this table. They were all his best friends. They were our best friends. Alan. Fred. Matt Selkowitz and his pregnant wife.

Matt Selkowitz waved. "Hi, Ame! Long time no see!"

"I know," I said. "Hi."

Then there was silence. I looked at Josh and Tessa.

"Congratulations," I said.

They nodded. They were both smiling the kind of gentle smile you might use when you gave a homeless person a dollar and said, "Take care of yourself," the smile that said, "Don't use this all on Boone's Farm strawberry wine."

Alan put down the butter. "So, Amy, how you doing?"

"I'm doing well," I said. "How you doing?"

"Great!" he said, and hugged his girlfriend, Janine, who, like everyone else, was in the middle of eating the fish course. "I got my girlie here. We got some good chow. What could be wrong?"

"What could be wrong?" I said. I was having a full-blown panic attack and I was in desperate need of a Valium, but what could be wrong?

“Baby, hand me that piece of rye bread,” Alan said to Janine.

“Well, okay,” I said, waving. I looked at Josh and his wife again. “Congratulations,” I said. “Congratulations.” And even though I wanted to stop saying congratulations, it kept coming out.

When Phoebe and I left the restaurant, we both held up our right arms to hail her a cab. “What a fucking disaster,” I finally said. “I just kept repeating ‘congratulations, congratulations.’ I wanted to be Princess Grace, to be elegant under fire, but instead I was crazy Princess Stephanie, the one who joined the circus. I was such a loser. You have no idea. I felt like everyone was like ‘Oh my God, what’s she doing here? Who invited her?’ ”

“I’m sure it wasn’t as bad as you think,” she said.

“You’re right,” I said. “It was so much worse.”

The cab came and she hesitated getting in.

“Go, please?” I said, pushing her in. “I’ll be fine. Really, I want to see this movie, and more importantly, I don’t want to go home. Now, go.”

“I’ll have my cell on,” she said and pulled away.

Walking over to the movie, I thought: “Where can I find someone like me?” Not exactly like me, but someone who had my values. My loyalty. My friend Ray went to Egypt with his hot, Swedish girlfriend, who contracted a serious case of dysentery. He had to make adult diapers out of bedsheets and then bribe a cabdriver to take them on a twenty-four-hour ride to a hospital in Israel. The doctors said he saved her life. I would do that. I wanted someone like that. Someone who would sleep on a damp hospital floor if I was in a coma. Maybe even someone who would consider joining the Peace Corps in her sixties like Miz Lillian, Jimmy Carter's mother. I realized that was my problem: I wanted me, even though, at this very minute, I couldn't stand to be with myself.

I got to the movie, and there was already a modest line an hour before the next show. I took my place behind two girls, who, from what little I could pick up, were college students at NYU. The shorter girl had frizzy, sandy hair and delicate freckles that were scattered along the bridge of her nose like stars. The taller, darker one smoked a clove cigarette, savoring her freedom away from home. I looked at these girls who possessed the kind of innocence that you could have only once in a lifetime; they squealed and fluttered their hands when a truck backing up made a popping sound. I thought about myself at their age, how I thought I knew everything about relationships, and how slowly, with each year, I'd come to think I knew less and less. I was reminded of my boyfriend at twenty-five, a self-described nature lover from Minnesota, who moved with me to Los Angeles when I went to graduate school to study screenwriting. He felt about Los Angeles the way some people feel about being swarmed by killer bees, and although we were still very much in love, we broke up. He was the one who taught me that you could love someone, and it still might not work out. Then there was the boyfriend who loved Salvador Dalí, the Union Square Cafe, and anal sex. I explained that I was not a fan of the latter. I said that although I'd never tried it, it always made me think of the calf pictured in the PETA ad, whose eyes are popping out of its head as it looks desperate to escape from its tiny cage. I remember thinking, "Is this a deal breaker? It's just one thing, after all." But he mentioned it more and more, talking about an old girlfriend who'd worn a plastic plug called an "ass expander." He said she wore it every day at the office when she worked at *Mademoiselle* magazine. She came to love anal sex, he said. Eventually, I said, "Okay, fine. I'll do it if you give me an epidural and afterwards I can wear a strap-on and do it to you." I thought that was funny. He, not so much.

Once inside the movie theater, I took a seat on the aisle, since the movie let out after midnight and I was planning to make a run for a cab afterward. I wanted this night to be over. It was a small room, narrow, with maybe a hundred seats, tops. The movie began with a scene of a young boy standing at a spelling bee, contorting his face wildly as he tried to think of the correct spelling for a word. As the movie progressed, it became clear that the winner of the national championship would not necessarily be the one who wanted it the most or even the one who studied the hardest. It might not even be the boy who planned to feed an entire village in India if he won. He's the one I wanted to win. The movie seemed to say that winning or losing comes down to something random—something beyond our control. Many kids said they knew all the words but the one they picked. They did everything right, everything they could have possibly done, and even then, it all came down to dumb luck. And although I loved the movie, this was the last thing I wanted to hear.

· 8 ·

WHO THE HELL IS GEORGE?

I WENT TO a small private school in Manhattan where the male teachers tended to resemble the cult leader Jim Jones. They dressed in strange combinations of clothes, as if they had flown cross-country and lost their luggage, which was why the new biology teacher, Mr. Lemmler, made such an impression. He had a trim, athletic body, curly hair the color of cornflakes, and a kittenish smile. He brought glamour to our dingy, poorly ventilated halls.

"I saw Lemmler on the porn channel," Isaac Powell announced one Monday at lunch. He patted the few hazy whiskers above his lip, the ones I suspected he darkened with a black eyebrow pencil. Either that or he'd used his napkin to clean out an exhaust pipe. "It was a commercial for an orgy, and he was having sex on the floor with, like, fifty people."

In the late seventies, on Fridays only, soft-core porn was shown on Channel J at midnight. I had seen it only once and very briefly. Channel J was a strictly low-budget operation. The lighting was grainy, and interviews were often conducted in the nude on a dirty, tattered mattress. The episode I saw featured a drowsy stripper whose breasts flopped just above her cesarean scar.

"You must have made a mistake," I said, looking across the cafeteria at Mr. Lemmler, who was sitting alone, thumbing through a textbook and taking tidy bites of his cherry pie. "It wasn't him."

"It wasn't he," Isaac said, invoking a rule of grammar we'd just learned. "And it was and he was going wild with these two chicks with circus tits." He grinned. "There's a reason he teaches biology."

As the rumor grew, inquiries were made, and a few weeks later, the news came out that Mr. Lemmler had forged his teaching credentials. Apparently he not only looked like a movie star, he was one, featured in films with titles like *Star Whores*, *Charlie's Anals*, and *Saturday Night Beaver.*

Years later, I would remember this introduction to Manhattan cable television when I got a job appearing on a local show called *New York Central,* a breezy half hour dedicated to all things New York. I was reminded of Mr. Lemmler, because so often when I told people about my new job on cable TV, they joked, "Are you on the porn channel?"

In addition to the gossip columnists, the theater and restaurant critics, the fashion expert, and the music guy, I covered single life in the city. So far I'd done stories on a bingo night at a Brooklyn bar with "winners, losers, and people just looking to score!" (this was the kind of sassy voice-over we used on the show); sung a karaoke duet of "Don't Go Breaking My Heart" with an older, Chinese alcoholic who belted out "Don't go baking my art!"; and interviewed a Hare Krishna who said the best way to meet people in New York was to dance in traffic.

At thirty-six, I'd never been on camera before appearing on *New York Central.* I'd dreamed of being on television for years, watching interview shows and thinking, "I wish I could do that. I could do that!" But since I'd thought I was too old for television at twenty-five, at thirty-six I figured I had about the same shelf life as a gallon of milk.

The executive producer of *New York Central* had read some pieces I'd written about dating, and when I went in for the interview, he offered me the job on the spot, even though I didn't know how to hold a microphone, let alone speak into it. I got an agent, an enthusiastic young man named Barry, who wore large, square, oversized glasses like an elderly movie tycoon, and said things like "I see big things for you! Everybody's looking for relationship experts!" Which led me to wonder, "Relationship expert? Do you mean me?"

. . .

TONIGHT I WAS with my young producer, Ned, and the cameraman, Tony, filming an event called "Get Drunk and Paint!"—a mass painting party at an art gallery on lower Fifth Avenue. This was the kind of "being single is fun!" story we did on the show. I had never viewed being single as particularly enjoyable myself; in fact, just the opposite. Once, when asked to describe how fun being single was, I mentioned *Looking for Mr. Goodbar,* the story of a lonely teacher with scoliosis who cruises singles bars desperate for companionship and is ultimately murdered. "There's a single story for you," I said. In addition, I rarely went to parties anymore, unless they were for one-year-olds. As a result, the fun single world that we covered on *New York Central* was as new and exotic to me as it was to anyone.

The art gallery, a loft, had a long, rectangular table in the center crowded with jars of tempera paints, empty bottles of rum, and tall sleeves of Dixie cups. The walls were lined with plain, white paper. Heavy drop cloths blanketed the dark wood floor. As brisk electronic music played, groups of people stood painting flaccid flower arrangements and multicolored handprints. The crowd was almost uniformly stylish, young, and attractive, with lots of culinary fashion—spaghetti straps, muttonchops, and meaty, palpable lust. Often when we filmed these stories, I caught myself staring, fascinated by people who actually seemed to enjoy being single. The more I studied the women in the room, the more I became convinced that they knew what they were doing. They knew what they wanted and how to get it. They were on a mission, while I looked as if I worked at one, dressed in a baggy gray, Ultrasuede blazer and formless brown pants. This was part of my problem. I'd thought I looked kind of sexy and chic when I left the house, when I actually looked as if I were in a bad high school production of George Orwell's *1984*.

"Okay, so I set up an interview for you with the gallery owner," Ned told me. Ned was in his mid-twenties and looked like the kind of handsome, spiky-haired college student you might see in a Girls Gone Wild video. He'd be in the giant crowd scene, gently layered with strands of shiny, plastic beads, yelling "woo hoo!" and "partay!" while raising a warm cup of beer.

He continued speaking, pointing to the corner. "And then I thought we could interview those people over there and—" He stopped and watched as a girl in combat boots and jean shorts walked by, her plump bottom sticking out from under the frayed edges. "Jesus. That is just so right on so many levels."

"That's less than I wear in the shower," I said.

I wasn't kidding.

We watched as the young woman swayed down the stairs, the confident pivot of her hips. I unbuttoned my lunky blazer, feeling about as alluring as an older Margaret Mead.

The first person we chose to film was a giddy young woman wearing a gauzy shirt and Wagnerian braids. She was painting a desert "flower," her version of a Georgia O'Keeffe that was, on closer inspection, clearly a vagina with teeth.

"Is this a good place to meet someone?" I asked, holding the microphone just under her chin, but not too close to her mouth.

"Oh my God! What could be more visceral and bonding than creating art together?" the young woman said into the camera. A streak of cracked red paint adorned her bare shoulder. "Everyone here has paint all over their hands, all over their skin. The paint is wet and greasy. It's just so . . ." She smiled seductively, nibbling the end of her paintbrush. "So magical. So primal and sensual, really."

"Thank you, that was great," I said, and as we were walking away, I turned to Ned. "Well, she's getting laid tonight."

"Oh, definitely," he said, yawning. "Last night Todd and I," he said referring to his roommate, "met these really cute girls at the Raccoon Lodge and yeah, yeah, anyway when they woke up they were hungry."

"For another blow job?" I said.

"Well, yeah, and some pancakes, but anyway, I'm completely beat. They were cute. You didn't do anything last night, did you?"

After two months, he knew me well. "I got into my pajamas at seven. That's something."

"Cohen, I keep telling you, you've got to come drinking with us. I know you think you're too old, that all the guys would think, 'Who's that old lady?' but—"

"I'm begging you. Please. No more."

The reason I never went out with Ned and his friends was

that I felt about going to bars the way my childhood pet rabbit felt about being dressed up in doll's clothes. I hated bars. I was afraid I wouldn't know what to say if men came up to me and even more afraid of how I would feel if nobody came up to me. I told people I didn't like bars because I was afraid of meeting a guy who would impress me with his knowledge of John Cheever, talk tenderly about his family canoe trips, and then show me his extensive collection of leather hoods and discipline paddles. But, when it came down to it, it was really the idea of rejection that scared me the most.

Next, we filmed a chubby guy with glasses who was painting a chubby guy with glasses. He was standing alone in the corner, occasionally adjusting the strap of his overalls, which he'd paired with a white tank top that exposed his slack, woolly shoulders.

"Is this a good place to meet people?" I asked. This was the question I posed in every interview.

"Hell yeah! Can't you tell?" he said, pointing to the empty space around him. "I'm a regular Mr. Popular. Ladies love me."

"Ouch," Ned said as we walked away. "That's the kind of guy that screams: 'The last time I had sex I needed a credit card.' "

I knew this guy would never make the final cut. Our goal was to show fun places where people could mingle, find love, and live happily ever after. And he just didn't sell it. He was more like one of those glum men you would see in a commercial for a potent antidepressant, the one with the soothing voice-over that says, "Do you dread waking up in the morning?"

We moved on to two men who weren't painting, but instead finishing up the last drops of a two-gallon jug of wine.

"Is 'Get Drunk and Paint' a good place to meet people?" I asked the taller man. He was one of those inscrutable, hip downtown types, who looked as if he could be a music mogul, a dot com impresario, or just live with his parents.

"Well, yeah. Duh." He grinned. "Hello? Getting drunk is always a good start."

"For him it's the only start," his friend said.

"Let's get a shot of you painting something," Ned said, leading me to a clean sheet of paper. I did a woman's face, dabbing bluish pink for the cheeks and green swirls for the hair. In high school, I'd produced several paintings of women as vegetables and fruit. One pensive woman sat in front of a mirror, her body an avocado. Another woman was a strawberry. This was meant to symbolize their fragility and how, like overripe produce, women are easily bruised. That's the kind of fun girl I was in high school.

"Hey, the dating chick isn't bad," the young man said. "Hey, dating chick. Nice painting."

"Thanks," I said and walked away. "The dating chick?"

"That guy was into you," Ned said.

"No, he wasn't. Was he?" I looked back at him. "Is that flirting?"

"It was so obvious," he said. "Your painting wasn't that good. Come on, you should know these things. You're the dating expert."

I'd been referred to as the dating chick. The dating expert. The dating diva. I'd always thought the word "diva" meant an actress who demanded sushi on the set for her chihuahua. I didn't take the labels seriously, because the whole idea that I could be an expert was, well, insane. But recently I'd been getting the idea that there were people who actually believed this afforded me some level of expertise. I'd written a bunch of pieces about dating, which was really just my way of asking a large number of people, "Is anyone else as confused and frustrated as I am? Is anyone else having this much trouble?" I was saying that I felt as if I knew nothing about dating, and the irony was it had somehow led to my being called an "expert."

Ned elbowed me. "That guy's still looking at you. Just turn around."

I did, watching as the young man gave his friend a noogie.

"He's a child. I'd feel like Mary Kay Letourneau," I said, referring to the Seattle teacher who'd had an affair with her sixth-grade student. "What would we have to talk about?"

"Who said anything about talking?" Ned said. "You've got to start having more fun. Live a little."

I'd heard this a lot, that I should be having more fun, and I never knew how to react to it. I was reminded of a time years ago, when, on a mountain hike, my boyfriend urged me to "relax" as we made our way down a particularly steep, rocky stretch. As someone who's terrified of heights, who gets dizzy standing on second-floor balconies, I was feeling great that I'd made it that far without shitting my pants. "Just relax," he said, standing over me, as I slid down a jagged embankment on my ass. "Don't you think if I could, I would?" I said. Which is exactly what I wanted to tell people now.

I GOT HOME at around one, too wired to sleep. From my window, I looked at the soft, fuzzy lights illuminating an empty Lincoln Center. My building was silent: the guy next door wasn't having loud sex with one of two Croatian blondes, who would later discover each other and have a loud shouting match in the hall; my upstairs neighbor wasn't pacing the bare wooden floor in what sounded like tap shoes. This was exactly the kind of night that made me think, "If I'm such a dating expert, why am I a thirty-six-year-old woman living alone in a dark apartment?" If I were more fun, I could have stayed at the party. When we left, it was just getting going. People were gyrating as if they'd been taught to dance by Caligula. They weren't going home alone. Just me.

I was reminded of something my friend Ray told me. "If I saw you on TV, I'd think you were getting boned left and right. I mean, you're on TV, for chrissake. It's a giant personal ad, and you're just wasting it!" Another friend, who had just gotten married to her boyfriend of seven years, put it more bluntly. "Fuck everyone," she said. "I mean it. What could be more liberating?" Even my father seemed to think I was having more sex than I was actually having, as I'd learned recently when he phoned to suggest an idea for my next article.

"Sweetheart," he said, "why don't you write about when you go to a bar and meet a man and then go to bed with him a few hours later? Write about that."

"But, Dad, I've never done that."

"Are you sure?" he said. "I could swear you told me you did. You sure you didn't go to a bar and then—you know?"

"Yes, I'm sure. I think I'd remember that."

"What about that blond guy a few years ago from Minnesota? Didn't you meet him in a bar?"

"I met him at college, and we were friends for months before we even kissed."

"Sweetheart, you seem to be getting very upset about this. You're not a child anymore. You're a grown-up lady. You're human and everyone has needs and we're all adults."

"Fuck everyone." "We're all adults." These were the kinds of comments that made me wonder: "Am I going to regret not having more sex?" I'd been thinking this for a while. But I also knew casual sex wasn't for me. It never had been. I got hurt if someone didn't call after we'd just kissed. When things didn't work out with someone I liked, the only comfort was saying, "At least we didn't have sex." People accused me of having high moral values, but the truth was I had a low threshold for pain.

Just before three, I got ready for bed. I did not slip into a come-hither, ostrich-trim nightie, but instead wore the kind of bulky separates that looked as if they had been issued at a Soviet work camp and were meant to be worn with a babushka while digging for cabbage. On nights like this I told myself I was relieved to be alone, and sometimes, I even believed it. I brushed my teeth and, still wide awake, sat down to check my e-mail. And there it was: George87634. The e-mail address I secretly hoped to find every time I turned on the computer. George Milzoff, the man I'd recently called "The perfect man for me. If only he were available."

"It's late and that's why I'm not calling," it began. "So it's finally done. Jane and I broke up. I moved out most of my stuff today and I thought maybe we could get together for coffee or even dinner? Are you free tomorrow? Love, George." I'd had an aching crush on George for close to five years, since the time we sat next to each other at a birthday dinner and he told me he thought the sitcom I wrote for was funny, "but not the kind that makes you laugh." I found him dark and smart, and I loved his long eyelashes, which were like awnings shielding his blue eyes. He was the one my friends dubbed "The Rock Star," as he played guitar in a popular alternative rock band that favored the kind of quirky, ironic lyrics my friend Eve called "exhausting." Once, when I was still writing for television, someone told me they'd heard George and his girlfriend might have broken up, and I'd schlepped down to his midnight show dressed in a flaming red half slip. "Oh, hey, Amy," he said. "My girlfriend likes that thing you're wearing."

As potential mates, I'd long thought musicians were about as dependable as meth addicts and bounty hunters. For one thing, they tended to be "edgy," a quality I once thought meant "iconoclastic" and "original," but which I now realized was really just a more creative version of "damaged" and "unlikely to call back within seventy-two hours." And now he signed his e-mail "Love." Not "Best" as he had written when he thanked me for a condolence card I'd sent when his mother died, but "Love." I wrote back and made a plan to meet the following night after work.

THE NEXT MORNING I arrived at *New York Central*'s studio on Bleecker Street. It was a loft decorated to look as if you'd dropped in on an impossibly chic friend who favored bold blocks of color and touches of fifties kitsch. Today when I arrived, Ned greeted me by putting his arm around my shoulder.

"Hello, my little tulip," he said, giving me a squeeze.

I backed away. "Oh no. What is it?"

"Buttercup of my garden."

"I'm worried."

He nodded. "They had a meeting about your hair."

The "they" to which he was referring were the executive producers of the show.

"They had a meeting about my hair?"

"The hotel piece," he explained.

A week before we had done a story on the ten-year anniversary of a posh Manhattan hotel in midtown. Many celebrities had been invited to the party, and I was told to look my best. I spent hours getting ready. I wore a fussy, plum-colored camisole with a lacy edge and wide black pants. I blow-dried my hair and sealed it with spray. In fact, everything was proceeding perfectly, until the camera crew was an hour late, forcing me to wait outside during a thunderstorm with no umbrella. As a result, by the time I yelled, "Donald! Donald Trump! Over here!" the lingering humidity had made my hair look as if I'd been gently electrocuted. You know you're in bad shape when Donald Trump needs to give you hair advice. Years later, he would use the same disapproving stare on *The Apprentice,* just before shouting, "You're fired!"

As we watched the footage of the party together, my executive producer, Rodney, shook his head. He was a thin man with bushy brown hair cut in the style of a seventies pop star, and droopy, doleful eyes, which made him appear sad even when he was smiling. Recently, he told me that before this job, he'd worked at a tabloid in England that prided itself on getting nude photos of celebrities on the beach.

"Amy, do you like this job?" he said.

"I love this job," I said. "I love it. I do. I used to dream about doing what I'm doing now. I love talking to people. I could do it all day. I do do it all day."

He waved his hand toward me, gesturing for me to calm down.

"Okay, okay. I got it," he said. "But if that's how you really feel, I'm not going to hold anything back." He motioned to the television. "For God's sake, you can't even brush that hair, you'd need a rake. And what's that?"

I looked closer. "Mascara smeared on my chin?"

"And look at your T-zone shine. It's blinding." He put his hand on my shoulder. "Darling, get the makeup they use to cover stretch marks and burns."

Rodney was aware that I had no previous on-air experience and that I was learning as I went along, which was why he often reminded me that he was not criticizing me in these little chats, but instead simply pointing out the way things were done. He made it clear he was trying only to help when he said a certain pleated skirt was so bulky it made me look as if I were wearing a colostomy bag.

"There's something else I want you to see," he now said, leaning over to sort through a stack of videotapes.

"Great," I said, worried he might produce a clip where my nipple was showing.

Rodney fast-forwarded to a piece I'd done on a hula hoop contest at a bar called Tortilla Flats. We watched footage of dexterous hips gliding in easy circles, many keeping the plastic sphere afloat for several minutes.

"You think hula hooping died in the fifties? Well, think again," I said, microphone in hand, straining to be heard over the crowd. My smile was broad and determined.

A winsome, button-nosed blonde appeared next. "Hula hooping's all in the gyrating," she explained. She wore a cropped T-shirt that showed off her immaculate, porcelain belly. "You just go around and around and around with your hips. Pushing and swinging and pushing. I can do it for over an hour."

"I'll bet you can," Rodney said.

"How long could you keep it up?" I asked a flush young Irishman. "The hula hoop, I mean."

Rodney smiled. "Good. You're keeping it sexy and tarty."

"I could keep it up all night," the Irishman said, winking into the camera.

Rodney pressed "pause."

"See, that's good!" he said. "All these randy, young people in a smoky bar in New York City, hungry to rip each other's clothes off. That's what people like to see. They want to see other people having the sex they wish they were having. Going home and rocking it until the bloody morning! It's selling the fantasy. Understand?"

I understood the fantasy very well. There was actually a time I got excited at being single. In my more fantastical moments, I imagined nothing short of a baptism. I would be invited to parties where I would play charades with Moby and Marc Jacobs. I would meet lawyers who could play "Purple Haze" on the accordion and made their own sushi. These thoughts faded quickly, making way for the hope of just meeting someone nice and good, someone who made me laugh and with whom I could "just relax." But now I found myself wondering if maybe even that very simple wish was the biggest fantasy of all.

Rodney sat on the edge of the desk, his arms folded. "Amy, for God's sake, you're supposed to be our glamorous single girl in the city."

I glanced down at my outfit, a ribbed khaki tank top pared with jeans.

"Glamorous? Have you ever met me?"

"Very funny. Glamorous. Got it? And by the way, no more bloody jean jacket. Every time you're in a piece all I see is jean jacket! Jean jacket! Jean jacket! You dress like Billy bloody Jack! It's not glamorous."

"Okay, no more jean jack—"

"Don't you have any designer clothes?" he said, sounding exasperated.

Designer clothes? Unless the designer he meant was "The Gap on sale," I didn't think I could afford it on what I got paid.

"I know you don't like to hear it," he said. "But people think being single is glamorous."

"Clearly, these are people who aren't single."

"Glamorous," he said. "You live a glamorous life. And not so much nodding when you do interviews. It looks like you have a bloody disorder of the nervous system. Like you're in the late stages of Parkinson's!" He gave me a quick pat on the back. "But otherwise, keep up the good work!"

LATER THAT NIGHT, I met George at a Thai restaurant in Tribeca. It was a muggy June evening and he was wearing loose, plaid Bermuda shorts, a threadbare Motorhead T-shirt, and a brown wool cap.

"You're wearing a wool hat in ninety-degree weather?" I said.

"I'm an idiot," he said, removing the hat and running his hand along what was now only a trace of blond hair.

"When did you shave your head?"

"Umm. A year ago? We were in Helsinki and I lost a bet."

He hugged me with one arm, holding his beer with the other. I could feel a spongy layer of flesh covering his bones. We sat down and began the jumpy, halting conversation of two people who sort of knew each other, but not really.

"So tell me about the fabulous rock star life. Any groupies? Have you smashed any hotel rooms?"

"Ha. Yeah, right. Lately, we've played lots of cities where Mennonites are within cart distance," he said. "You know, Lancaster, Pennsylvania, and parts of Ohio. That's as wild as we've gotten. We did a few TV spots in L.A. to promote the new album."

"And? Was it great?"

He exhaled, rolling his eyes.

"Not really. I mean, it's great before you go onstage. Then you're the king. The host says he loves your album and plays it in his car. The network executives come shake your hand. But the second you're done and they're on to the next guest, you're like the weird cousin with the cheesy smell. No one gives a shit about you. You're nothing. But, everyone's been telling me I sound bitter, and that's why I've started taking yoga, even though I hate that faux-spiritual, 'how's-your-practice,' harmonic-conversion, 'the-universe-is-in-order' bullshit."

"He's adorable," I thought, looking at him. Girls must throw themselves at him all the time. I bet they hide in his tour bus and surprise him wearing only their school rings. Sitting there, I found myself growing simultaneously attracted and defensive.

George waved his hands in the air. "I mean, why can't yoga just be about the workout? Why does the teacher even need to mention being a vegetarian or tell us not to litter? And why do we always have to say good-bye in Hindu? Do I sound really bitter?"

"Just incredibly," I said, smiling.

We sat there in silence, and as we did, I tried to downplay my fantasies of traveling with the band. Of standing just offstage at a large, muddy music festival in Scotland, wearing rubber Wellies and a miniskirt, my legs far longer and skinnier than they were now, watching George do his five-minute solo, with our new baby in my arms, its ears protected by special kiddie headphones.

"I've read all your articles," George said. "I thought of writing and telling you that I liked them, but I was dealing with my situation and you know." He shrugged. "Whatever. I didn't. So what's it like being a dating expert?"

"You do know that's not me," I said, looping some pad Thai around my fork. "I'm in there, but it's an exaggerated version of someone who's not exactly me. I mean, those articles are fun to write, but I always think I sound much more cynical than I am, because I'm not cynic—" I took a moment to figure out what I was trying to say. "It's creating an idea of something. I mean, I don't think of my life as glamorous either. It's a character."

He looked confused. "But they're nonfiction, right?"

"Well, yeah, they're true-ish, but they're not diary entries."

"But every artist struggles with that."

"Artist? I write these little pieces about dating. That's not art."

"Why? You're commenting about something in society. When Andy Warhol did the Brillo boxes, it was art. I'm not saying you're Willa Cather, but you're creating something, so I think you can call yourself an artist."

"Not with a straight face," I said.

I had to be careful with this one. I didn't want to be some flash in the pan. God, I was old. Who used phrases like "flash in the pan"? I'd started to say a lot of things that made me feel old. Things like "You're thirty-three! I should be carrying you in a BabyBjörn!" and "I've had this dimple on my ass longer than you've been alive." I'd also noticed that recently I'd become more sensitive about my age. A few weeks before, when I was walking along Houston Street, a young man called out, "Looking good, Mama!" And all I could think was: "Mama? What happened to Baby?"

We finished dinner and took a walk down West Broadway. As we crossed Leonard Street, he put his arm around my waist in a very relaxed and familiar gesture. It was the way you'd hold your girlfriend of five years, not a girl you'd been with for less than five hours. What was I doing? This guy wasn't ready for anything.

"I want to see you as much as possible," George said, kissing me.

We began making out. "Go home," I warned myself, although what I said was "Me too." As we continued, I thought about how to tell him we needed to take things slowly. We needed to go slowly if we wanted this to work. But there wasn't any "this" yet. If you use a word like "this" too soon, it sounds an awful lot like "us," which sounds even more like "One day soon I'll be weeping in your bushes with binoculars." Maybe I could just not say anything and leave, thus sending the message that we should move slowly. Then George looked into my eyes and said, sweetly, "Before I go away."

"Go away?" I said. "Where are you going?"

"Los Angeles. To house-sit for the summer. Basically, it's one long, two-month mooch, but we've got a bunch of tour dates in Japan, so I can just fly back and forth from there. I'm leaving tomorrow, which I now kinda regret. But I'm going to be in touch very, very soon."

After that, we spoke constantly. While he was waiting at LAX for his luggage. When he was buying a black bean quesadilla at Whole Foods in Santa Monica. When he was just back from a yoga class, worried that he'd pulled his groin. We spent hours on the phone every day, all of which led me to wonder: "Am I nuts? Who gets involved with a musician just out of a five-year relationship?" It's like the relationship version of giving a chimp a loaded gun. You know you're going to get killed; you just don't know when. But then two weeks later he called and said: "Hear that? That's fifty thousand screaming fans! I'll call you when I get to Tokyo!" I knew I was hooked.

I WENT TO Saks to find the sort of heavy makeup Rodney had suggested. If you've never been to a cosmetics department in a large department store, you should know that you risk being exposed to one of New York's most bitter subcultures: out-of-work actors. This was why I walked quickly, darting from counter to counter before anyone could say, "I have just the thing for your blotchy skin!" I was dashing from NARS to M·A·C, when I heard someone call out, "I know you! You're on TV!"

The woman was leaning over the eyeglass counter, her elbows sinking against the glass. She had shoulder-length black hair held back by a velvet headband and excitable blue eyes that seemed more piercing because she was so tan, which also made it hard to tell if she was in her thirties or forties. Her pale yellow, crewneck sweater revealed a white Peter Pan collar and a short strand of pearls. I assumed this was the kind of woman who loved horses, her old sorority sisters, and the Yule log.

This was my fan. I had a fan.

She waved me over. "Hi, Amy. I'm Peyton. I watch your show all the time. I love you. You always seem to be having so much fun. And I especially, especially loved the story you did on bikini waxes."

I'd interviewed a woman about Brazilian bikini waxes, and upon hearing that the mostly Russian aestheticians asked their clients to get up on all fours so they could more precisely wax the anus, I said, "That's a hell of a way to get a green card."

"I could so relate because you just feel so much cleaner without all that hair," Peyton said. Even her whisper was manic. "Plus, it makes such a difference sensitivity wise. Right?"

"You know, I want to try it, but I never have."

"Oh my God, shut up! Go out and get one right now! It changed my life. Do you have a boyfriend?"

I thought about my phone call with George the night before, when he told me he would be stopping in New York at the end of July, on his way to a wedding in London. "I have a six-hour layover and I want to come see you," he said. I was thrilled, but yet again, I told myself to be careful. It's a layover, which meant he probably just wanted to get laid. But then we discussed his emotional trip to the Museum of Tolerance, and whether Al Gore was condescending, and if the *Los Angeles Times* compared to the *New York Times*. And I thought, "You don't discuss the Museum of Tolerance if you just want sex. If you just want sex, you discuss the Museum of Modern Art maybe, but not the Museum of Tolerance. Maybe he was just in the wrong relationship for five years. Don't be so cynical. He's coming to New York just to see you. If he just wanted to get laid, he had Los Angeles, a city filled with sexually enlightened young women who carry around fur handcuffs and enough condoms to moonlight as drug mules."

"I think I have a boyfriend," I now told Peyton. "But he just got out of a long relationship, so I'm being very careful."

"So smart. Women need to be so careful because we need to protect our inner wolf and preserve our fierceness," she said. She bent down beneath the counter and stood up holding a photo. "This is my old boyfriend. Beyond gorgeous, right?"

He actually was. He was dark and angular, with loose, wavy hair that framed his reluctant smile.

"He's Latvian. When we met, he didn't speak English. At first it was hot, like, we don't need words, but then, it's like, you're with someone who can't communicate with the world. It's like dating Helen Keller. So I made him learn. Anyway, we just broke up after five years."

"Oh, I'm so sorry," I said.

"Don't be. You know why? He was a sex addict. I love sex. I'm multiorgasmic, but twice a day should be enough. Because after a while it's like any addiction. It takes over. I started getting movie tickets in advance so I'd be sure we'd go, but even then, he'd want to have sex as we were leaving. And I was, like, 'Compromise. A quickie?' And he always said yes, but he never could. I mean, I know some women would die to have that problem, but I never saw *American Beauty*. I never even saw *Titanic.* And I love movies. And I love sex. I'm multiorgasmic. But then I started thinking about all the things I could have done with that time. I could have learned Kabbalah. Or taken a cooking class. I'm multiorgasmic, but I just couldn't take it."

"Oh yeah" was all I could manage before she interrupted me.

"So, any advice?" she said.

When I first started writing articles, I got a letter from a woman who asked if I knew a good restaurant in the Village for a second date. I thought that was a difficult letter. Then a prisoner at Rikers Island wrote me. "I think we might have a lot in common," he said. "People think I'm really angry too." He was in for attempted murder. Now, granted, his letter was much more whacked out than the others I got, which tended to be so plaintive and sincere. "I meet people, but I can't keep them. Help!" "I'm shy, so I come across as a bitch. What should I do?" "I'm terrified I'm going to die alone. Any advice?"

I thought of an e-mail I'd received from a young woman in Las Vegas. "As you write about dating," she said, "what do you think I should do about this guy who insisted on introducing me to his parents and then broke up with me because he said I was getting too serious? I've been on so many dates and I just don't know what to do anymore." I wrote back saying, "You have to believe if he wasn't the one, there's someone else out there." "THERE'S SOMEONE ELSE OUT THERE." I wrote all in caps. "OUT THERE." It sounded as if I were referring to a different galaxy. And maybe I was. We were all so confused, drifting in darkness. I wanted to tell these people, "Honestly, I feel the same way. If I didn't, I wouldn't be writing these things. I'd be at home with my family, feeling sorry for people who had to go out on dates."

Peyton continued. "Don't you think he has all the signs of addiction? He thinks he's just a horndog, but come on. Right?"

There was a substantial pause. "I don't know," I said apologetically. "I don't know anything. I think you need to ask a professional."

"Aren't you a professional?" she asked. Her look of confusion faded quickly. "Oh, well, that's okay, you're close enough."

TONIGHT, NED, TONY, and I were in a vast, lime green room in midtown. We were doing a story on a "speed flirting" class led by a woman named Karlee Bailey, who introduced herself as the dean of the "University of Love." She was a vivacious, moving palette of bright pinks, rhinestones, and cascading brown hair that fell in donut-sized ringlets.

"Flirting is a language just like French or Chinese," Karlee explained in her frilly Southern accent. She was probably in her mid-fifties, and waved with all her fingers pressed together, rocking her wrist methodically. It was the wave, I thought, of someone who'd competed in small beauty pageants, the kind meant to encourage the local economy, with contests like "Vermont Cheddar Princess" and "Miss Detroit Hospital Supply."

The group sat at mismatched metal desks, listening eagerly, among them a giggling Japanese girl with a misshapen glass eye, a gray-haired man with severe acne scars who wore a cardigan buttoned snugly around his plump midsection, and a dour Indian woman who fiddled constantly with her sari.

"What a bunch of freaks," Ned whispered. "Are we at a *Star Trek* convention?"

"I know. I thought I was a dork," Tony said, moving his fanny pack farther back on his hip. "I'm glad I'm married."

I had suggested this story, thinking it would be funny and light. I thought we would film me trying to flirt, and I would make jokes about how I didn't know anything. Recalling this now, I wondered whom I'd expected to show up for a flirting seminar that cost fifty dollars. I was reminded of a time when I lived in Los Angeles and a group of friends suggested going to amateur night at a strip club in the valley. "It'll be fun!" they assured me. What none of us expected was a parade of desperate women too strung out, old, or out of shape to be professionals. As we were driving home, my friend said it best: "Well, that was about as hilarious as *The Deer Hunter*."

Karlee was now sitting in a metal chair at the front of the room. She was wearing a loose, pink silk shirt and appliquéd jeans, which emphasized both her femininity and her sense of fun.

"I've often thought we should petition the UN to make flirting the international language of the world!" she chirped. "Because you could be dropped in the middle of Africa or Greece, or even Tibet, and if you look longingly into someone's eyes, you don't need words."

She'd assigned us each a partner. Mine was a gaunt man wearing a short-sleeved dress shirt, his hands wriggling in his pleated khakis.

"I'm," he said, looking at the floor, "I'm, um, I'm Owen?"

“I like your shirt,” I said, as we’d been told to start our flirting with a compliment.

“This shirt?” Owen held a piece of his shirt, rubbing the waffled fabric between his fingers. “Thanks. Thank you. This shirt has texture. I read in *Maxim* magazine that women like clothes with texture. The undershirt has some texture, but not as much texture, as . . . um . . . um . . .” He squinted and gnawed at his lip.

“The other shirt does?” I said.

“Yeah.” He exhaled, happy to have said anything at all.

Watching Owen, I recalled moments when I felt this uncomfortable myself. The time in high school when I gained forty pounds, wore my hair in a bowl cut, and went on a date with a freshman at Yale who claimed not to know I was his date when he left with someone else. The more I thought about this, the more I realized I didn’t need to go back twenty years, I just had to go back a few months to my date with a man who seemed distant when we had coffee and told my friend afterward that he didn’t want to go out with me again because I was thirty-six and he wanted a lot of kids.

Karlee led us through several “double take” drills. This involved making eye contact with someone, looking away quickly, and then looking back at them almost immediately.

“Make eye contact, Myoko!” Karlee told the girl with the glass eye.

“I am,” Myoko said.

This was the first story we’d done that didn’t feel as if it were about dating, but something far more ominous: real loneliness. In the same way you can walk into a crowded room and sense tension or even the smell of sweat, the loneliness in this room was undeniable to the point of being oppressive. It was the kind of loneliness that could drive a person mad, the kind that made the world seem tiny and desolate. I knew this kind of loneliness myself, although I tried never to think about it, for fear that it would bring me back to feeling so desperate and lost.

"You might have to get home by yourself tonight," Ned whispered.

"Why?" I said.

"Because I think I'm going to kill myself."

I laughed, but what I was really thinking was: "Am I going to end up like them?" A few bad years, some bad luck, some bad decisions, a bad perm—it was possible. And while I could joke about it, I was starting to think there was the distinct possibility I could end up alone, like many of these people. I'd woken up mornings with this fear. Occasionally even in the middle of the night, my heart drumming.

"Hey, are you okay?" Ned asked.

"Why?" I said.

"You're sweating a lot," Tony said. "You might want to powder your T-zone."

"Here," Ned said, pulling a travel brush out of his pocket. "Rodney told me to bring it for you on every shoot."

"Listen up, people!" Karlee called out. "We're going to the bar soon."

"Thank God," Ned said.

For the final exam, the entire class headed to a nearby T.G.I. Friday's. As someone who hated bars, I could only imagine how it felt for a class of pathologically shy people. The bar was crowded with people who looked as if they went to Daytona Beach every year for spring break, even long after they'd graduated from college, nostalgic for bikini foam parties, unlimited Jell-O shots, and streaking contests. These were people who viewed flirting as a game, unlike the people in the class, who feared rejection the way some people feared needles or heights. Perhaps to protect themselves, the class remained tightly clustered in a dark corner so close to the kitchen entrance that every time a busboy came out of the swinging doors, the entire group shifted to the left.

Karlee urged the group to go mingle. "Use your lines, people!"

She was referring to the "ice breakers" she had taught us earlier. "For example: Go up to someone and say: 'Is there anybody in your life who would mind if I sat with you right now?' And if they say, 'My wife would mind,' then you know they're married."

The bus driver raised his hand. Earlier, Karlee had told him he needed to work on keeping his nose and ear hair neatly trimmed.

"What if they say, 'Get lost, you asshole'?" he asked.

"You don't want to be with a woman who curses," Karlee said. "Okay, everyone! Come on! Let's flirt!"

The class nodded, but no one moved. Finally, after a prolonged pep talk, the bus driver bravely approached a buxom young redhead, who dashed away when she saw him advancing. The only person who seemed to be doing well was Myoko, who had not one, but two suitors, both navy men wearing their sailor caps.

Owen didn't say anything for a moment, instead making tiny circles in the carpet with his shoe, as if he were stubbing out an invisible cigarette.

"Do you have a boyfriend?" he finally asked.

I was struck by a thrashing, beating surge of panic. Was George my boyfriend? Would I have to endure getting over someone else? I couldn't bear the thought of that.

"I do," I said.

"We made a bet. Not if you had one, but if I had the nerve to ask." He laughed uncomfortably. "So I guess I won."

I wondered if Owen, who seemed kinder than so many other men who were born with more confidence, would ever find love. Would anyone ever see past his lantern jaw and clumsy mannerisms to the sweet man underneath? I thought about this, and the more I wondered, "Is he ever going to find love?" the more I wondered: "Am I?"

"Jesus, you look terrible," Ned said. "Wanna leave?"

I waved good-bye to Owen. He was standing at the far end of the bar now with a bookish Filipino man and the older Indian woman, who was finishing off her third bourbon. He held up his hand to wave, and it was only after I waved back from a distance that I realized he meant it as a high five, and that I was supposed to walk over and slap his hand victoriously. I could tell he felt humiliated, as if everyone in the dark bar had witnessed the missed signal and viewed it, like him, as rejection.

"Good luck, Amy," he called over.

GEORGE CALLED ME from the airport and said he was starving. We made plans to meet at a Middle Eastern restaurant in the East Village where you could sit outside in the garden under the Christmas lights they left hanging year round. And where he could smoke. A month before he told me he'd started smoking again. "It's probably just my reaction to the breakup."

"Hey, baby," he said, walking in. "I missed you."

"Me too," I said, feeling very bold. I was scared to say this because I was still trying to be careful. But lately I'd been wondering where being so careful had gotten me. In my silent, dark apartment alone? Maybe I was too careful. I wished I were the kind of woman who would whisper, "The bathroom's free," and then lead George in there for a quickie. But who was I kidding? I was barely able to manage "me too."

He had a little more hair now, just enough to glisten along his scalp, and was wearing silver-rimmed sunglasses with blue lenses that looked better suited to an Italian playboy named Gianni. He smoked Marlboro reds between bites of fresh pita and told me more about the wedding he was attending.

"He's a hedge fund guy. She's a former lesbian."

I smiled. "I know so many men now who are dating former lesbians, I've started to think I should have a brief lesbian relationship myself in order to find a boyfriend."

"As long as I can watch." He leaned back in his chair. "You know I want to get married. I want to have kids and have a girl who's my best friend. I dig that shit."

The dialogue in my head protested my innocence: "It wasn't me. I didn't bring up marriage." Apparently, somewhere along the line, in spite of my best intentions, I'd bought into the idea that you should never talk about marriage too early if it's something you wanted. This was one of those moments when I realized that my emotional baggage, once a few neatly packed pieces, was now like the Joads' truck, stacked high with old clothes, half a rocking chair, a mule, all barely secured with twine.

As we shared a platter of lemony hummus and ate pita pizzas that arrived on warm wooden boards, I wondered if maybe the marriage comment was his way of telling me I was his girlfriend. Not his wife—I wasn't that crazy—but his steady. His main squeeze, as they used to say.

"I'm getting my own apartment when I move back in September," he said. "And I'm going to need help, so maybe you could come with me to Ikea."

"Yeah," I said, picturing not only the modular couch we would buy, but the drive to New Jersey, and perhaps even the lunch of Swedish meatballs.

After dinner, we had an hour left. We made out in front of a cemetery on Second Street, between First and Second avenues. A gray mist hung softly, and it was all very sweet and romantic. George held my hand, swinging it as we walked to get him a cab.

"You know how I feel about you, right?" he said. "I've told all my friends, but you know, right?"

I had no idea, but I said, "Yes."

"I'll call you as soon as I get to London." He looked at his watch. "In, like, ten hours." And then, he kissed me good night, and I never heard from him again.

A FEW DAYS later, as I walked around dazed and confused, wondering if I'd be better off without him, it was hard not to be struck by the symbolism of George's and my last moments being in a cemetery. How fitting, I thought. And that's when it occurred to me that even though I was still checking my phone messages and e-mail as often as a woman in labor monitoring her contractions, I was not completely surprised by everything that had happened. Somewhere I had known this was coming all along. Maybe I was an expert, after all.

· 9 ·

AN ELEPHANT IS AN ELEPHANT

RECENTLY, I WENT for a mammogram. This was not my first, as I'd had a false alarm at twenty-five when I found a firm, peanut-sized lump under my arm. At the time I was living in Los Angeles, a city that is to buxom, young blondes what the Galápagos Islands are to birds. This was why, even though I got my test at a major teaching hospital, my technician looked as if she could be serving tailgate buckets at Hooters. When I untied my gown, revealing myself to be naked from the waist up, she clapped.

"I'm psyched!" she squealed. "You're so flat! You're going to be so easy! The last woman I had"—she cupped her hands and let them sway and dangle around her waist—"was, like, huge. It was a nightmare. And the woman before her was, like, a B cup, but you're so flat! You made my day!"

My more recent technician was also young, with a sweet, earnest voice. She wore a lab coat over her neat, black clothes, and her hair was slicked into a serious-minded bun. After she told me my result was fine, she sat down to fill out some papers. As she did, she sighed loudly. I asked what was wrong.

"All my friends are getting married," she said. "I'm worried. I'm the only one left."

"Really?" I said. "How old are you?"

She shook her head, woefully. "Twenty-six. Why? How old are you?"

"Mmmm. Thirty-eight." I reached over to her. "You have nothing to worry about. Trust me. Absolutely nothing."

She asked me if, at her age, I had worried about ending up alone.

"Well," I said, a little too brightly. "Apparently, not enough."

The fact was that I had started worrying, really worrying, that I might actually end up alone as it dawned on me that my once irrational fear was slowly becoming a reality. Apparently, without realizing it, I had been assuming that I would eventually settle down by age thirty-six. Latest thirty-seven, but it would never come to that. That was just crazy talk. I figured I'd be on my own for a few years, just long enough to hone my independence on trips to Cuba, Vietnam, and the hardware store, and then I'd find my great love. But now I was two years over my limit and counting.

The first time I got really nervous was at my friend Madeline's party for her son's birthday, a large gathering where guests, many of whom I'd known from college, were encouraged to bring their young children. A whole room in the apartment was partitioned, crammed with a musical Jumparoo, a sticky alphabet mat, and something called the "Baby Einstein Activity Center," a learning toy meant to encourage innovative, complex thought, on which all the babies punched and drooled.

I tried to spend time in the children's playroom, but it was cramped, and no one offered to let me hold their screaming toddler, so I just stood there smiling and nodding and repeating, "What a cutie!" I eventually moved to the buffet table, where I met Gert, an aggressively tan woman who had just lost her husband to a stroke on the golf course, and a shy aunt named Rhonda, who told me, in her barely audible, evaporating voice, that she had been divorced over fifty years before. Rhonda wore large, round glasses and her long hair piled over her face. She carried herself like someone who assumed that even after you'd met her ten times, you'd forget who she was. Gert was bolder and, at two in the afternoon, on her third gin and tonic. She wore a gray flannel ensemble—turtleneck and pants—with chunky wooden jewelry that clacked loudly every time she moved.

As my friends launched into a hearty version of "Where Is Thumbkin?" in the next room, I sat on the couch with Gert and Rhonda, talking about the state of the Democratic party after Bill Clinton.

"The problem for the Democrats is the word 'liberal,'" Gert said. "It used to mean having a conscience, and now the Republicans are using it to mean 'communist,' as if having affordable health insurance is somehow un-American."

Rhonda agreed.

"Oprah should run for President," she said, softly. "She'd win easily. Did you see her show on makeovers for women over fifty?"

"It's so true," Gert said. "You can have ten women in a room who don't have anything in common—religion, race, class, even where they stand on abortion—but they'll all agree on Oprah." She pointed her finger at me, her nails painted in a pale salmon. "I'm old enough to be your grandmother, but you and I agree, don't we?"

"I like her," I said.

"It's true," Rhonda said. "There's nothing more unifying than Oprah."

Now the other room was singing "Old MacDonald," loud mooing followed by quacking. Two women I knew from college walked toward me, hunched over their little boys, who tumbled forward. They looked alike, these young moms—trim and bookish, wearing sweatshirts that could endure spit-up and juice spills.

"Hi," they both called over.

"Hi," I called back.

The women continued down the hall. One of the little boys started to cry and his mother scooped him up.

"Who's a Mr. Whiney puss?" she said, kissing him.

Gert turned to Rhonda. "Do you think I should redo my kitchen or get another face-lift?"

The conversation continued until I realized that I felt more comfortable with a widow and an aging divorcée than I did with many people my own age. Once I had viewed women like Gert and Rhonda as "those people," unlucky women who had somehow found themselves alone, but now I wondered, were "those people" actually "my people"? Had I already become one of "those women" without knowing it? I'd always imagined that ending up alone was a sluggish, steady process, years of ominous warnings that were ignored or even flouted, but now I was starting to think that maybe ending up alone was like getting your wallet stolen. Something that leaves you asking, "Hey, wait a minute, when did that happen? I was looking the whole time."

Apparently I had been fearing this for longer than I realized, as I'd noticed a change recently in the way I joked about being single. I used to talk about searching for love, saying things like "I want to find an older man who wouldn't have considered me in his prime." And "I'm starting to think that when people refer to the 'great depression of the thirties' they're talking about my thirties." But lately I joked about ending up alone: I had visions of myself living in a single-room occupancy hotel, obese from a steady diet of government cheese, wearing a muumuu stained with cheap wine and tears, while banging on my wheelchair with a spatula. I would joke about this to friends, pretending that

I was kidding—a muumuu, ha!—but the truth was, ending up alone was as scary as anything I could imagine.

Adding to the problem, when I typed the words "famous unmarried women" into Google, the words "Famous Old Maids" came up, which included a website called "Famous Freaks." Among those mentioned was "Lucia, the Puppet-Lady," who was, at one time, the smallest woman in the world, weighing "less than most cats." She was unmarried, which was how she came up in the search, but she was also "surprisingly happy for someone so small" and among the highest-paid midgets of her day. Another website referred to unmarried women who were "handpicked by God." As I read on, I realized that these women are often referred to as nuns. All of which made me realize that if I were going to be alone for a while or even longer, I had to find a way to picture it that didn't involve a traveling sideshow or a lifetime vow of chastity.

I decided to take a trip. It wasn't the romantic getaway I'd dreamed of: the tour of French vineyards, where a sommelier says, "We enjoy za wine now and zen later time for love. No?" But it was something. I chose a week-long bike trip to the Canadian Rockies, riding from Banff to Jasper. For many people, this would have been a refreshing, even challenging exploration of vibrant mountain terrain, but since I'd learned to ride a bike only three summers ago and still didn't know how to stop once I was in motion, it had the potential to be the kind of free-spirited, good fun that would land me in a full body cast. For life.

In the years since my mother died, my father had traveled many times with groups. On one trip he went to the Galápagos Islands, which he called the "Gapapagos" and which he described as "Fine. It was a nice trip. It was a bunch of birds." This was only his second vacation without my mother, and at the time, I remember wondering how she would have described the same adventure. She was a woman who would call and say, "I was walking down Lexington Avenue today and I happened to look up and I saw the most unusual and creative fire escape!" And now I could only imagine how she might have described the Galápagos Islands. "The tortoises have these voluptuous shells, and thick, lumpy ankles that look exactly like mine!" I imagined her laughing at her own joke. Then, knowing her, she would have added some peculiar detail like "And today I bought a banana from a toothless woman with the most exquisite feet!"

LOOKING THROUGH THE brochure of my bicycle trip, my father told me what to expect when traveling with couples. "After dinner, these people don't want to sit around and fumfernick with you," he said. "They might act like they want to talk to you, but that's only because they're polite. What they really want to do is go to their tent and relax, spend time with each other, so bring a good book."

On his first trip as a widower, my father had gone on safari with a company known for its ability to deliver luxury in even the most remote locations. A friend of mine went on a similar tour and said during dinner there were several men in sheer, white robes whose sole job was to shoo away all the monkeys. When my father returned, he was eager to show me his photographs, proud not only that he had gone all the way to Kenya, but that he had finally learned how to use his point-and-shoot instamatic camera. We sat at his dining room table, surrounded by sleeves of photographs, as he took me through his whole trip.

"Here's a zebra drinking," he said, pointing to what looked like a faint, marble rye in the middle of some tall grass. "Here's a lion sleeping. Here's an elephant by a tree. Here's another elephant by a tree. And there's me with the rest of the group. All couples except for that one lady I told you about."

He moved on to the next roll.

"Here's me with the Masai tribe," he said, showing a picture of himself surrounded by African women wearing layered cotton shawls in various shades of mustard and stocky brass neck rings that saddled their clavicles. "They're no dummies, the Masai," he explained. "For years they had all these tourists bothering them all day, so they got smart and decided to start charging five dollars per picture." He flipped through the remaining roll. "Five bucks," he said. "Another five bucks. Another five dollars and this one's blurry!"

He slipped the photos back in their envelope.

"I liked the trip." My father shrugged. "But after a while an elephant is an elephant."

. . .

On the plane to Calgary, I sat next to a woman in a mandarin-collared business suit, with pale, chubby hands she couldn't keep still. She fiddled with several different ways to roll her blanket into a bolster that might support her lower back, which she rubbed while groaning loudly. She went through a dozen sleeves of sugarless gum. She fluffed and poked at the manic black curls that rose out of her head like flames.

The pilot introduced himself in a round Southern accent as "Cap'n Dave." He said that we should consider the flight crew our family in the sky. Then, in what was clearly an effort to put everyone on board at ease, he launched into a rousing version of "Oh Susanna" on the harmonica. The entire cabin erupted in lingering, grateful applause.

Smiling, I said to the woman next to me, "That was so great, wasn't it?"

She shrugged. "Yeah. I guess so. I just hope he's not drunk. You know, a lot of pilots are alcoholics."

She confessed that it was her first time flying since September 11 and she was very nervous.

"Usually I really, really, don't mind flying," she said. "But today I feel a little jittery? You know what I mean? I'm sure part of this has to do with the media and how susceptible I am to the images they dictate? But I just feel . . ." Her voice trailed off. She put her index finger into her mouth and bit off the nail and then, with the tip still glistening with spit, held out her hand to shake. "I'm Gail, by the way," she said, swiveling her body so that she faced me. "Can I use your pillow? I just can't seem to get comfortable."

She went on to describe the many health problems she had endured over the past year. They were minor things, she said: a tipped uterus, persistent disc problems, an allergy to pigeons. This was when I realized that as bad as it is to sit next to someone who wants to chat the whole flight, it's even worse to sit next to someone who, it seems, wants a hug. "This poor woman," I thought. That is until she said, "Are you traveling alone too?"

And there it was: the word "too." As in "also," as in "Look what we have in common!" I wanted to say, "No, no, no, please don't lump us together. My compassion for you is based on pity, not camaraderie."

"Sort of." I explained that I was beginning a bike trip with a group the next morning.

"You didn't want to bring a friend?" she said sharply.

"I wanted to go on a bike trip, and none of my friends could go. I didn't want to wait."

She fluttered her eyes. "I'm sure you get this all the time too, but everybody tells me they can't understand it. They say, 'What is wrong with this world? How can you be single? You're a beautiful, smart, intelligent, vivacious, sensual woman.' And I say it's not me, it's the men out there. Do you get that all the time too?" She pointed at me and then back at herself. "I mean, you and I aren't supermodels, but so what? We're in the top . . . like, twenty percent, right? And that should mean something."

At that moment, had the plane's door not been so tightly locked, I'm fairly sure I would have jumped.

I got to Banff late in the afternoon. The July weather was perfect, a warm and windless day turning into a crisp, gentle evening. As a kid who grew up around concrete, once saying, "Nature's fine for some people, but it's just not my thing," it was hard not to be awed by the sublime beauty of Banff. It is a remarkably scenic little town, surrounded by tall, grassy peaks tipped with snow.

For dinner, I chose a restaurant with a lively outdoor balcony, which overlooked the main street below, with its peppy Swiss chalet architecture and rugged couples strolling in matching ponytails. In the right mood, anything can make you feel more alone, and this night was no exception. I was nervous about my motel room, with its flimsy door, perfect for someone who didn't want to fiddle with a lock when he could be hacking me to death with an ax. I was nervous about eating dinner in a place I didn't know. Perhaps this was why when the hostess asked, "Are you just one?" it got to me. Just one. This is when you realize that "just" put with anything is never good. "Just" belittles anything it touches. Just friends. Just looking. Even "just a million dollars" suggests you were hoping for more.

"Yes," I said. "Just one."

The hostess was probably twenty-two, tall, with a jagged, bleached pixie cut and wispy legs that were spaced so far apart

I wondered if each knew the other existed. She led me past the crowded dining area to what was essentially the single room occupancy section of the restaurant, a group of lone adults positioned far away from the families with jumpy, small children.

A man with blond dreadlocks jogged after his little boy, who was running with a chopstick held above his head like a spear.

"Come back, Montana," he called, catching the boy by the waistband of his dungarees just before he entered our territory. "Those people didn't ask to eat with you."

Those people. There it was again.

My friend Ray once told me that the first few times he ate dinner alone he felt he needed to bring a prop, a book or a pad of paper and pens, so that he could jot down very important things and look ensconced in his rich inner life. I had forgotten my book in my room—a Dorothy Parker anthology, which included the story "Big Blonde," about a desperately lonely woman who's passed from man to man until she ultimately tries to end her life with pills—and only had my cell phone, which I placed on the table as if to announce, "Look, everyone, I have friends. Somewhere."

It wasn't as if this was the first time I was dining alone; I'd eaten by myself lots of times, but when I worried I might be eating this way for the rest of my life, my independence started to feel more like a liability. On that balcony, I had the sense that I was facing something that terrified me. I felt like someone who's afraid of heights and confronts it by going to the top of the Empire State Building and peering over the ledge, except this was a fear I was meant to face calmly, even cheerfully. I was choosing to be afraid, I was even told on occasion. "After all, if you wanted to, you could always find someone. Lots of women are taking trips to Alaska these days."

I'd read about a study that said that people who thrive on danger—skydivers, ice climbers—often produce a natural opiate that masks their terror. The more they confront danger, the less they feel it. If only, I thought, that worked for me. These days when I heard the song "Eleanor Rigby," with its chorus of "Ah, look at all the lonely people," I practically needed a Xanax.

I observed my fellow solitary diners as the ghosts of Christmas future, all cautionary tales I was meant to heed. Looking at them, I started to wonder how each came to eat alone. There was the man who sat Indian style in his chair, one hand tugging at his beard, the other turning the pages of *Carl Sagan's Cosmic Connection: An Extraterrestrial Perspective*. I imagined he'd been in love once, with a math major who shared his passion for the Monkees and Dungeons & Dragons marathons. She hurt him and now he was done. Aliens were much easier to understand. Across from me was another man who, it appeared, had fashioned himself as a kind of Burt Reynolds in Santa Fe, down to his woolly, plaid blanket jacket, Frye boots, and stiff, puffy toupee. He was divorced, I thought, at least once. Maybe he liked the falling-in-love part, but grew tired of the work that came later. He actually seemed like a perfectly nice guy, smiling and lifting his ceramic beer stein in my direction, but I looked away, as if to say, "No way, buster. You're not getting any of this," ignoring for the moment that he hadn't even asked. At another table, a dour redhead isolated parts of her salad, scratching the fork against her plate, so that the beets and onions were in a kind of ghetto along the edge. I pictured her online personal ad filled with so many exclamation points it looked like there was a picket fence after each sentence: "I LOVE FUN!!!!! I LOVE SUNSETS!!!!!! NO SMOKERS OR DRINKERS!!!!! WHERE HAVE YOU BEEN ALL MY LIFE!!!!" I wondered if she scared men, revealing too quickly that she used to pluck out all her eyebrows in high school, and commenting that these days, everyone she knew was being diagnosed as "bipolar." "It's this year's Epstein-Barr," she said.

Were these my people?

I guessed they were, as much as any married person has something in common with another married person. I wondered which of these people considered themselves in transition—"I'm alone until I meet the right person"—and which had resigned themselves to a solitary existence. In the past few years, I'd found that whenever I mentioned the possibility of ending up alone, it was usually met with "Don't be crazy. Of course you'll meet someone," or from my friends who were worried themselves, "Please don't even say that word. I'll stick my head in the oven right now."

My friend Ray admitted that he saw his life as a string of

women who never quite understood him, but were perky and let him do whatever he wanted until he moved on. He said he hoped he died quickly—in a car accident or skydiving—because the idea of dying alone was the one part that really worried him. When I asked my friend Eve if she ever got nervous, she said, "It's age. I started worrying when I turned thirty-seven. You wonder if you'll always be alone because you've gotten so used to it. It's scary and weird because you're living it, but also trying not to think about it because if you thought too much about your life you'd never get out of bed." We were on the phone and she sighed loudly. "If only I'd been blessed with lower standards. I'd be a happier person today."

I maintained that part of the problem was that my generation didn't have many single role models. Growing up, I knew of only three women who were unmarried. The first was my mother's friend, Eden Levine, who always traveled with a padded photo album featuring professional snapshots of her cats posed in costume.

"Here's Fluffy as a bandito," she said, looking tenderly at a plump Persian wincing under the weight of a sombrero. Then she showed us a photo of a deeply aggravated white American shorthair. "And here's Spongecake as a bride," she said.

Breezing in for a weeklong visit, Eden always seemed so glamorous. I remember once saying in awe, "Eden is so pretty. She looks just like a stewardess." Her hair was the color of a lemon left out too long in the sun, and her thick, white lipstick shimmered. She always dressed in short-sleeved leisure suits and smoked cigarettes as long as drinking straws, which added gravel to her powdery, girlish voice.

The second unmarried woman was my friend Jackie's beautiful godmother, Denise, who sported lime green hot pants I initially mistook for underwear. She maintained it was her part-time job as a cocktail waitress that afforded her a huge apartment off Fifth Avenue, with a vast, mirrored ceiling over her vibrating round bed and several different boyfriends who called every ten minutes to make dates with her. The third was my Hebrew School teacher, Miss Yarone, whose overbite was so pronounced that I often feared that as she ate her egg salad sandwich, she might accidentally bite through the ample flesh of her chins.

In the same way you might go to China, meet a handful of people in a country of one billion, and think, "Oh, so that's what the Chinese are like," these three women were my ambassadors from the land of the unattached. It never occurred to me to feel sorry for them, with the exception of Miss Yarone, but only because she was entirely unprepared for how restless a group of eleven-year-olds could be. She learned quickly not to let us take our coats, scarves, and book bags when we said we were just going to the bathroom. She was also the one who confiscated the thick ham-and-cheese sandwiches we brought to a Yom Kippur service.

In the weeks before she stopped showing up, Miss Yarone quit trying to teach us Jewish history, preferring instead to teach us about life. She told us that Israel was essential to the survival of the Jewish people, and that Tel Aviv had some of the best health clubs in the world. She told us about her favorite singers.

"My favorite is Barbra Streisand," she said. "You know if she had lived in Nazi Germany, she might have been gassed."

To which one of the girls in class responded, "God, Hitler was so obnoxious!"

Miss Yarone also told us about her search for a boyfriend. "The mens here only want one thing," she said, securing the bobby pins around her short, stringy wig. "They want bing, bang, bong, good-bye. In Israel, men don't mind a fat wife because they just want to live in peace."

As a child, I could sit on my bed for an entire afternoon wondering, "What would it be like if I had to use my feet as hands?" I saw myself in the supermarket, hopping through the produce aisle, lifting a heel up to sort through some cherries, and at home, getting a callus on my big toe while writing a thank-you note. I could picture every detail of that life, but I still couldn't fathom what Miss Yarone did on weekends. What did you do if you had no one to do it with? In the rare moments I did try to picture her on a Saturday night, I always envisioned her as an Edward Hopper character, sitting in a dimly lit apartment, on a shallow cot in a half slip, listening soberly to the lively sounds of the street outside. This was my vision of a woman who lived alone. And now I couldn't help but wonder: Was I going to become one of these women? Did some little girl think of me as her Miss Yarone or Eden Levine?

. . .

I MET MY group the next morning in the dark, chilly dining room of a motor lodge. A round of quick introductions followed. The Fabers were finishing up omelettes that looked like yellow, mangled sleeping bags. They were traveling with their two freckled teenage boys, both as long and lean as pipe cleaners. Jenny from Chattanooga waved along with her husband, a lanky kidney specialist named Eugene. Kip and Dot were there to celebrate his seventy-fifth birthday.

Although I tried not to, I found myself thinking in terms of The Group and me. The Group is packing up their bikes and I'm still trying to adjust my seat. The Group took all the granola bars, and now I'm stuck with the ambrosia with the flaccid coconut. The Group is taking off without me. The Group doesn't seem to notice I'm not with them. Now I can't even see The Group, and it's just me on this scenic, but desolate and drizzly, road.

I'd experienced this isolated feeling many times. A boyfriend of mine once told me he thought it was because when I was in first grade, I was put in the slowest reading group. Originally, I assumed I would be placed with the best readers, Mindy Weinstein and Mark Negropont, who also happened to be the most popular and the best athletes in the class. Instead, I was put with a girl who'd stuck a bobby pin into an electric socket and a boy who, it seemed, had no understanding of the word "soap." I went to my teacher, Mrs. Stevens, arguing that a mistake must have been made, and she assured me that no, my reading was actually that bad. Unlike the other groups, each of whom had their own shiny Formica table positioned around the classroom, our group met outside on the stairs, sitting in single file so people could go up and down more easily. This, my boyfriend said, was the beginning of my life as an outsider. "That's when you started thinking in terms of you and them," he said. "That's what did it. You're fucked for life."

I arrived at lunch as the group was finishing up. The small campsite was nestled at the base of a lush, green canyon, surrounded by towering trees.

"We've been here an hour!" Kip said, waving to me with one of his delicate, liver-spotted hands. "We thought we lost you!"

"He's seventy-five and he beat us too," a woman named Candace said, sliding next to me at a picnic table. "I mean, it makes you wonder why you bother at all."

Candace and her husband, Louis, had driven up from Seattle, where they were visiting their new grandson. Candace's gray hair was short and choppy, and she wore the kind of wacky eyeglasses that avant-garde German architects tend to wear. The kind that say, "I'm creative!" I knew I liked her when she leaned over and whispered, "How many other Jews do you think are on this trip?"

I laughed.

"No, I mean it," she said. "You're the only one who's obvious. Cohen—that's an easy one, but the others?"

Louis chuckled to himself, patting his wife's leg. "She does this on every trip. You should have seen her at the Vatican."

Just looking at Louis, you could tell the nature of his and Candace's relationship. She was the wild one, and he, with his balanced smile and everyman haircut and clothes, was her rock.

Candace pointed to an older woman named Audrey, a creamy blonde who looked to be of Norwegian descent.

"I mean, clearly she's not a Jew, but there have to be more than three of us. Right?"

And just like that, it was the first day of camp. The first day of first grade. You make one friend, and you don't leave her side. Candace was now officially my best friend, even though she'd just asked if my name was "Emily."

In the afternoon, I rode behind her, squinting to make out the back of her helmet. I was feeling pretty good about keeping up with Candace until she told me she'd recently broken her ankle and it was still swollen.

The next day, the weather turned unseasonably cold, a thin frost covering everything, making the roads very dicey. Breathing, panting actually, as I pedaled up an eight-mile hill, I exhaled what looked like a fine mist of talcum powder. Since I hadn't prepared for cold weather, I was wearing all the clothes I'd brought at once: two T-shirts and two sweatshirts under a Patagonia fleece, green thermal tights under my long, padded shorts, a lavender bandanna tied around my head under my helmet, and gloves. Today we were visiting Lake Louise, which had the most beautiful water I'd ever seen, a glamorous turquoise poised against all the surrounding mountains, some transcendent in pine green, and others all granite except for a little white of fresh snow. It was at Lake Louise that I had the humbling experience of meeting someone whose dog was in better shape than I'd ever be.

"Mildew went on a nine-hour hike with me last Saturday," his owner said, patting the black Lab. He was the kind of guy whose bong was attached to the outside of his knapsack. "And we went on a sixteen-day rafting trip. He also loves to jog. He never gets out of breath."

This was all told to me as I reclined on a large boulder, wondering, after the morning's ride, if I'd ever walk again.

At dinner, I was seated across from Ted, a man in his fifties who was also traveling alone. He was a genuine loner, I thought, unlike me. I was faking it for the time being. He didn't need to make friends or fit in. He was happy leaving well before the group every morning and even happier never to speak to any of us. In cooking terminology, Ted had what would be called a dash or a pinch of hair and a businesslike stare when he addressed you. He didn't say much until the conversation turned to bicycle trips he had taken before.

"Every trip I've been on, someone lands in the hospital," he announced, slicing into his venison. "In Tuscany, this gal flipped over the handlebars, and when we flew back to America, no one was sure if she was permanently paralyzed or not. And when

I was in Belize, this fella had a heart attack. And in Africa someone got this fungus. At first, they thought it might be a version of the flesh-eating virus."

Candace nudged me. "He's a barrel of laughs."

Tonight, Candace was wearing a white smock over a loose, flowered dress. She told me it was a cheese maker's smock, which she had purchased in Paris. Looking at it, I was reminded of one of my favorite quotes, by the nineteenth-century food writer Jean Anthelme Brillat-Savarin, who said, "A meal without cheese is like a beautiful woman with only one eye."

"But then the fungus started to blister," Ted continued.

"P.S., Kate and Rodney," Candace said, referring to a bubbly, athletic couple from Newton, Massachusetts. "Jewish. They told me at lunch."

Ted then announced that he was off to bed. He wanted to get up before dawn. After Ted left, Jenny from Chattanooga said, "Do ya think he's gay?" She leaned forward on her elbows, resting her pale face on her fists. "Eugene doesn't think he's gay."

"He's gay," Candace said. "I think he's one of those men who is, but nobody thinks he is. The kind of man who constantly falls under the gay-dar."

"I didn't think Elton John was gay, so you might be right," Eugene said, reaching for the white bowl in the center of the table. "Is there an Equal packet in there?"

"What do you think?" Candace asked me.

"He could be picky," I said. "Or shy."

"Shy!" Jenny said. "I never think of that."

"He could be asexual too," Candace chimed in. "He's told me he spends a lot of time with his nieces and nephews."

Ten minutes before this discussion began, I'd been planning on going to sleep early, but now I wasn't leaving. What, I wondered, would they say about me? "Poor Amy, maybe she aims too high," they might say. "You know so many women her age have unrealistic expectations. Or maybe she likes the wrong kind of men. Or maybe she's bitter!" Recently, I'd seen a few of my single friends get increasingly bitter, growing weary and impatient with their lives, sniping at other people's good fortune because they felt so forgotten.

"I want to make the word 'victim' fashionable again," one of them said. "Feeling sorry for yourself is so out of fashion now, and I want to bring it back in a big way. I'm tired of looking on the bright side."

I'd seen them become more exhausted with each disappointment, angrier at a world that had let them down. I'd felt a little of the bitterness myself—never strongly, but the vaguest sense of not being completely happy for a friend who announced she was pregnant with her third child, when I was debating whether to try online dating. Bitterness now seemed like a world into which you could pass without even knowing it, just by letting your guard down.

After the dessert plates had been taken away, Jenny drank the last of her decaf. "Yer sa brave," she said, looking across the table at me.

I thought her response was to what I had said earlier about only recently learning to ride a bicycle. "That's very sweet of you," I said. "I must have been nuts to go to the Rockies on my first bike trip."

She wrinkled her pert nose. "I don't mean the bicycle," she said. "I mean because you came on this trip alone. I mean, I could never, never do it."

"Me neither," Candace said. "You are brave."

"I agree," Eugene said.

"You're so brave" can be interpreted in two ways. The first kind is what you might say to a fireman. This is the version that says, "I admire you. I'd love to be more like you." The other is what you might say to someone who was just in a terrible car accident but is making a full recovery. This is the one that says, "You make me feel better about myself, because I'm not you."

I didn't know what to say, and so I said, "No, I'm not."

"No, you are," Jenny said, shaking her head. "I just can't imagine going somewhere alone in a million years."

Candace nodded vigorously. "I look at my mother and I don't know how she copes with being alone all the time," she said. "Although she's getting senile. Which helps."

The next day we visited the Columbia ice fields, one of the largest accumulations of ice and snow in the Arctic Circle. There was an observation deck at the visitors center, where people stood admiring the dramatic expanse of ice in front of us. This afternoon, the group was scattered. Some were in the parking lot taking pictures. Some were signing up for the Sno-Coach tour of the glacier. Everyone else, exhausted from the forty miles we'd done that morning, had gone to their rooms upstairs at the Ice Fields Chalet.

"Do you want to watch TV with us?" Candace asked, noticing me standing alone. "We can put Louis on the couch, and you and I can channel surf and raid the minibar!"

It was such a kind and generous offer. How could I tell her that the mere thought of it made me want to drink my way to the Betty Ford Center.

"That's okay," I said, waving. "I'll see you guys at dinner."

Although it was cloudy all morning, now the afternoon sun had come out—smoky and vibrant orange—and with it, crowds of people, delighted by the warm weather.

"Right there is a slow-moving river of ice," a man told his young wife, who held his thick waist from behind, resting her head between his shoulder blades. "I read in my book how they look powerful, but actually they're totally fragile. Like, things die all the time, like the plants and wildlife, and sometimes you can hear avalanches in the distance. Survival is a daily struggle on those ice fields."

Standing there, looking at that desolate, frozen mass, I remembered my father saying about his safari, "After a while an elephant is an elephant." I wondered if he thought the elephant would have meant more if my mother were still alive. I could imagine her watching the elephants' enormous gray bodies, excitedly saying, "You know, they can live to be eighty!" and "According to the *Guinness Book of Records,* the largest elephant ever was from Angola and weighed twenty-four thousand pounds!" Or maybe she wouldn't have said anything, and they would have just stood there, silently, content that they were not alone in the jungle.

· 10 ·

THE ICE CLIMBER COMETH

I THOUGHT I'D never been better. Casual, chatty, barely letting on how unshakably neurotic I really am. We even laughed a little during that first phone call. William, my blind date, and I made plans to go to Chickpea, a tiny falafel place in the East Village. He told me he was six foot three, with dark, curly hair, and would be carrying a copy of *One Flew Over the Cuckoo's Nest*. "I'm teaching it," he explained. I started to describe myself, but then interrupted with a confident, dare I say plucky, "No descriptions. I'll find you. The place isn't that big." I thought it was a terrific first conversation. I'd never been better.

But, after dinner, when we sat at a murky bar drinking Bosnian beers that tasted as if they'd been brewed with kitty litter, William told me that not only hadn't he found me irresistible or even the least bit adorable, but he almost hadn't shown up. Apparently, until the moment he arrived at Chickpea, he was debating whether to cancel.

"I was this close," he said, his thumb and forefinger practically touching, "to calling you and bagging the whole thing."

"Really," I said. "What stopped you?"

"You got here on time," he said.

THE FIRST TEST in our new relationship came three weeks after William and I met.

"I'm nervous," I said.

"What's there to be nervous about?" he asked reassuringly.

"Well, you know. Just utter and complete humiliation."

At the time, William and I were deep in that "I can't believe I found you!" phase. The one where you say things like "You were suicidal in high school! I was suicidal in high school too!" Or "You're lactose intolerant? Me too! You get gassy with painful cramps? Me too! Don't you think that's amazing?" And so this first test made me nervous, as I worried that even the smallest things could taint our newfound bliss.

"Don't worry," he said. "It's just grammar."

"Ugh," I groaned. "My stomach hurts already."

What made the situation even worse was that I had actually asked to take this quiz, dared him to let me see how I'd do on the test he had recently given to his ninth-grade English students. After I finished, I handed him my sheet of paper, and he began marking it. I listened carefully to the scratches of his felt-tip pen. Was that the sound of a check? An X? A smiley face? He handed the test back to me.

"Five out of twelve?" I said, horrified.

I suddenly felt like one of those ditzy girls who, when asked if they wanted to see an exhibition of Dalí's surrealist paintings, say, "Dolly Parton paints?"

"Well, in a few cases you caught one mistake in a sentence but not the others." He pointed to sentence number five. "This should be whom, not who." He patted the top of my head, and I could feel the pity seeping into my scalp.

"Don't I get half a point for getting half the sentence right?" I tapped the page. "I got that comma right, and I hate to tell you, no one really cares about semicolons."

He shook his head of shoulder-length black hair, his dark eyes telling me, "Just admit gracefully that you failed. This desperate ploy for half points is a little sad."

"Don't worry," he said. "Besides, it's not like it was just you. The whole class failed."

"But they're in ninth grade!"

"WILLIAM" WAS NOT my boyfriend's real name. He asked me not to use his real name, and so we went about trying to find him something he felt suitably represented him, perhaps the name he'd wished he'd always had. A lanky Mexican from Northern California, he suggested I call him "Angel" or "Jesus."

"Or Puppet!" he said excitedly. "I knew a kid named Puppet when I was growing up, and he was a real tough motherfucker. Call me Puppet."

"I'm not calling you Puppet," I said. "What am I supposed to say: 'My boyfriend Puppet'? I'd have to call myself Geppetto."

He thought for a moment. "Then how about Che?" he said, as he is often told he looks like Che Guevara, although thankfully he would never wear a beret. "Or what about Noah? Or wait! Jonah, because I almost became a Jew."

Years before I met him, William lived on a kibbutz near Tel Aviv for several months, and as a result, thought seriously about converting to Judaism. "I just liked the clarity of Judaism," he told me. "Your God doesn't make you feel guilty or tell you constantly that you're going to go to hell. He just tells you what to do, and if you don't listen, you're fucked."

"Okay, Jonah," I said. "Are we going with Jonah?"

He thought for a moment. "No, hold on, is that a pussy name? How about something like Estragon or Godot because you've been waiting so long for love?"

"How about Siddhartha?" I said, referring to one of his favorite books. "I could make you a big stoner too."

"I was a big stoner."

"Then why don't I call you Roach Clip or Sensimilia? Forget it. I'm calling you Wally."

"Wally?" he said. "How about Willie? No, that sounds like the whale. Okay, William, as in William Blake."

"Okay, William," I said. "Fine."

THREE WEEKS AFTER the grammar debacle, forty days after we first met, William gave me another quiz. It was the morning after our first Valentine's Day. He told me that there was a present he'd forgotten to give me.

"What is a symbol?" he asked, as we stood wedged in my kitchen, which, while big for a Manhattan apartment, was about as wide as a photo booth. William was dressed for work, wearing a black sweater, dark jeans, and square, monk strap shoes. Thankfully, this morning he wasn't wearing the pair of shoes I'd joked were such a pale shade of brown they looked as if they were made of human skin. I, on the other hand, was dressed for a day at a "rest facility," the kind of place where I might be recovering from "exhaustion" on an "outpatient basis." My hair was in two husky braids, the kind I imagined would be worn by an elderly waitress at a German restaurant. I was wearing glasses, puffy slippers, a T-shirt speckled with coffee stains, and loose drawstring pants with a crotch that hung so low it looked as if I were concealing an udder. The first few times William slept over, I'd worn flighty camisoles and boy shorts, sneaking into the bathroom before he woke up to make sure my hair was a carefully disheveled yet hopefully sexy mess, but apparently I was now comfortable enough with him to walk around looking like shit.

"What is a symbol?" he asked again.

"Must we?" I said.

"Come on, tell me. What is a symbol?"

I looked at the clock. He had to leave in five minutes.

"What is a symbol?" I said, wearily. "Oh my God, I don't know. I don't want to do another test. You have to go. It's getting late."

"Just tell me," he said. "What's a symbol?"

"Honey, I'm getting colitis," I said, referring to the spastic colon that had plagued me briefly in high school.

But he stared at me, waiting.

"Um," I said. "Something that stands for something else?"

"Right," he said.

And then he handed me a small brown box with a willowy ribbon tied around it. I opened it and saw a small silver medal the size of a quarter. I recognized it as the one he'd worn around his neck for the last five weeks.

"It's a St. Christopher medal," he said. "I've worn it since I was twelve. St. Christopher carried Christ across water. Even when St. Christopher thought he might drown doing it, he got Christ to the other side." He smiled. "Like I will carry you across any water in our lives."

"That's so sweet!" I said, kissing him. "Thank you. I love it. Now get out of here. You're going to be late."

"Don't you know what I'm asking you?" he said.

"What?" I said, looking at the clock again. "It's almost seven-thirty."

"I'm asking you to marry me."

"You are?"

"Yeah."

"Oh my God. I was so excited we joined a gym together." I put my arms around his neck and began kissing him. "You're really asking me? Really?"

And it wasn't until a few moments later that we both realized I'd forgotten to say yes.

THAT DAY I called up both friends and members of my extended family. These were people who would have been ecstatic if I had called and said, "I have a boyfriend for the first time in six years, and it's lasted over a month!"

"Oh my God," they might have said. "Over a month! Let me sit down."

But now I had to call and say not only that I had a new boyfriend, but that we were engaged. I then explained to my Jewish family that there was no ring, and instead I wore William's Catholic medal around my neck, attached to a thin, leather strap. Most of their reactions went something like this: "Well, at your age, I bet you're just relieved you found someone."

With my friends, who had weathered my recent comments like "I've started to think that love is utterly random. Like winning the Publishers Clearing House Sweepstakes or being wounded in a drive-by shooting." With these friends, many of whom were still looking for love themselves, I called and announced, "There will be no lesbian commune for me." And then I added, "At least not yet." I either said that or "Good news! Hell has frozen over."

At a time when I had just started calling William my boyfriend (only weeks before I'd been using the vague term "seeing each other"), I was now reminded that he was my fiancé, a term I quickly came to hate, as it always sounded so self-conscious. Every time I said "fiancé," I couldn't help feeling as if I were really saying, "Look! You don't have to worry about me anymore! I know you thought I was on my way to becoming the eccentric aunt who looks as if she cuts her hair with a steak knife and asks to live in your basement, the one who seems to have fewer and fewer teeth every time you see her. Well, don't you worry another day. I found someone who wants to marry me!" And I think because there was some truth in this, it made me even more uncomfortable. Hoping to find a worthy substitute for "fiancé," I found myself using terms that were equally awkward, like "my old man" and "that guy who I'm planning a wedding with" and even the old standby from *The Newlywed Game,* "my hubby."

Even though William and I were now engaged, our relationship still felt very new. It was very new. I had only recently adjusted to the fact that William wore so many necklaces and trinkets around his neck that when he went to the bathroom in the middle of the night it sounded as if he were shaking a loose bag of change. Other times, it just felt as if I had a cat, whose tinkling collar allowed me to know its whereabouts. William was still adjusting to the fact that while he loved the outdoors, the woods and the beach equally, my idea of the outdoors was Union Square. And while he was an avid rock and ice climber, I had always believed that the word "ice" should be closely followed by the word "cream."

At this early stage, we were still filling each other in on all of our past relationships. William and I spoke now as if we'd been on a long journey that had finally come to an end, our voices etched with a sense of relief.

"There was this one guy I called the 'Bear Claw,' " I said. I bent my fingers and swiped at the air sharply. "I met him because Eve called and said 'I had a date with this guy who I found totally hideous—I mean completely repulsive, just the thought of being near him makes me really queasy—but you might be able to go there. Should I give him your number?' And I said yes and he was really funny and I liked him. Even though I didn't find him attractive at all, I decided to try. And we went out on a lot of dates and I was starting to like him more, until one night he came to my apartment and he was just sort of groping and poking—the man did not have a light touch—and, let me tell you, it was practically a clitorectomy."

"The Bear Claw," William said, laughing. "I love it."

We had names for the many women William had dated: "The Coat Check Girl," "The one with the beach house and the sex swing," "Mary Poppins," "Mrs. Butterknife."

We would sit on my bed for hours telling each other stories, more delighted with each new thing we were learning. In the six years I'd sat on my bed alone, this is what I dreamed a relationship could be. I never thought about dinners at hot, new restaurants or weekend trips to quaint inns with rooms that I would later describe as "Laura Ashley meets Miss Havisham." I just imagined someone I loved talking with, who made me laugh.

Of all the men I'd ever been with, William was the one with whom I had the most fun doing nothing. We both loved to meander, and could spend hours wandering around Astor Place trying on skull rings and answering the question "Which tattoo would you get?"

I realized just how comfortable I was with him one Saturday, when we went to a small brunch place on the Upper West Side, decorated with wooden cows and barn doors. We ordered apple pancakes and a spinach omelette and shared them both. Our waitress told us that P. Diddy, the rap mogul, was sitting two tables behind us, and we craned our necks to get a look. Afterward, I excused myself to go to the bathroom. If there's one thing I hate, it's a bathroom with a door that opens onto the dining room, because if the lock comes loose, you'll be caught with your pants down in front of a hundred people who only wanted a nice meal. These bathrooms made me extremely tense, which was why when someone kept jiggling the door, then tried to force it open, I got very nervous.

"Look at my ass," I whispered when I returned to the table.

"I think I might have peed on myself a little. I was crouched and this person kept forcing the knob, like they were going to break the door down. And P. Diddy's table was right there! How bad is it?"

I turned around to show William the back of my pale olive green pants, and as I did, I remember being so thrilled that I had a boyfriend with whom I felt so comfortable.

"Just a tiny, I mean, tiny bit." He smiled. "Honey, you can barely see it, but I know you, so let's stay until it dries." And then we ordered another omelette and a plate of banana French toast.

I ONLY WISHED my mother could have been around to see us. My mother and William shared a love of Kafka and Milan Kundera's *The Unbearable Lightness of Being.* I imagined leaving them alone to discuss eternal reoccurrence while I read *People* magazine in the other room. William would have appreciated my mother's kookiness: her penchant for kimonos and shoes with polka dots; her architectural tour of New York, which started at the Cloisters and ended in Chinatown, where, over a dim sum lunch, she would have encouraged us to try the tripe wontons. The more I started imagining my wedding, the more I found myself wondering what advice my mother might have given me about marriage. She was never pushy about advice, even when I desperately wanted her to be. When I begged her for her opinion—saying, "Just tell me! Should I move to

L.A. or not?"—she said I knew the answer and needed to come to my own conclusion, which drove me insane. Throughout my parents' marriage I'd seen them bicker constantly about everything from whether to take the Gowanus Expressway to my father threatening to throw my mother a surprise birthday party, at which point, according to her version of the story, she said if he didn't stop, she'd throw her drink at him. They were faced with my mother's many bouts of cancer and my father's long business trips, and through it all, they remained utterly devoted to each other, and I realized, that's all she ever needed to say.

WILLIAM AND I got plane tickets for California so we could go tell his family our big news in person. He didn't want to call them because he wanted to see their expressions. At forty-one, William was convinced his family had given up any hope that he'd ever marry.

"They're going to shit," he said. "They're not going to believe it."

At thirty-nine, I said my family worried about the same thing.

"Of course I worry about my thirty-nine-year-old unmarried daughter," my father had said a few months before I met William. "Wouldn't you?"

"Well, you never worry about Holly or Tommy," I said, mentioning my older brother and sister.

"That's one hundred percent false," he said. "I worry about

them all the time. I worried about Hol last year when she drove home in that terrible rainstorm. And I worry that Tom exercises too much."

When William and I were introduced by a mutual friend, it seemed incredible that we'd met each other at this point in our lives. Two months before, my sister had been diagnosed with breast cancer. When William and I had our first date, I hadn't been out to dinner in as long as I could remember because I had been going with her to every doctor's appointment and every chemo treatment. During the week, I often slept at her house in Scarsdale to help out and pick things up, and force her kids to bake cookies with me. William's father had been diagnosed with cancer too, the year before. This was why, in February, we began discussing wedding dates for May, when we knew his father would still be well enough to travel.

WHEN WE GOT to California, we picked up our rental car. It was a drizzly morning, the sun hidden behind a heavy curtain of fog. William drove quickly. When we got to his parents' house, an hour later, we found out William's father had lapsed into a coma. We knelt by his father's bed, his mother, sister, and nieces surrounding us, and William whispered in his father's ear that we were getting married. His father didn't respond, but took a deep breath that William's mother believed meant he understood the good news. She kissed us both and continued crying.

I was familiar with comas, having seen my mother slowly withdraw from the world herself almost seven years before. At the time, my only coping mechanism was to try to find the good in my situation. Sometimes I told myself I was channeling my ever-perky mother, who I was sure would have done the same thing; other times I called it denial, proclaiming my admiration for not facing the truth. Whatever the answer, I found myself saying things like "The nurses are so great!" (though they repeatedly ate all the fruit I'd hidden in the salad crisper) and, most often, praising my father, who, while often driving me crazy, cared for my mother beautifully. As her eyes glazed over and she didn't recognize us anymore, he became the cheerleader who said things like "I got you some nice tempura!" And "What a terrific T-shirt you have on! It fits so nicely! Isn't that something?" In William's mother I recognized this same version of love that was at once so mundane and so intense. Like my father, William's mother insisted on keeping her husband company, regardless of whether or not he knew she was there. She read *O, The Oprah Magazine* in a chair in the corner and tried not to doze off, even though she hadn't slept for days; she led relatives into the room and told them to speak up because maybe William's father could hear them. And just as my father and William's mother were cheerleaders for the people they loved, I now found myself doing high kicks and shaking my pom-poms for William.

"I just think it's so beautiful that the whole family is around your father's bed and they're all singing to him and stroking his head and telling him how much they love him," I said, trying to put my arm around him.

He pulled away. "Well, I don't think it's so beautiful," he said, his arms crossed tightly. "I don't see what's so beautiful about wearing adult diapers and dying in your own piss. You're lucky you can see it your way, but I don't."

We didn't leave the house all weekend, sleeping on the floor of the den when we weren't sleeping on the floor in William's father's room. We listened to William's father breathe, noticing as it got more shallow, but still he kept going. The nurses said he could stay like that for days. Even weeks. And then Monday night, two hours after we left his family's home to return to New York, we got the phone call that William's father had died.

William debated whether to stay in California. There was no funeral, but instead a memorial service scheduled for the following month, and since he was due at school the next morning, he decided it was best to return to New York.

ON THE PLANE ride home I did everything I could to cheer William up. I bought a copy of *Penthouse Forum* so we could read the letters out loud, much to the delight of the timid man sitting next to us. I told William about a girl I went to college with, whose name was Ima, and who had written an article for the school paper about household objects that could be used for masturbation. I told him we called her "Ima going to tell you everything you never wanted to know." For Ima, there was nothing in the house that was off limits if you wanted to diddle yourself: a bottle of Wella Balsam conditioner, a pair of sheepskin slippers, a whisk. I told him how I used to joke that if Ima ever asked me over for dinner, I'd insist on wearing a hazmat suit.

He laughed. And instead of leaving him alone in his grief and silence, I tried to make him laugh more. "At least no one's farting on this flight," I said, referring to our trip a few days before. At one point the smell became so overwhelming someone a few rows ahead of us shouted, "This is an airplane, goddammit! Not a toilet! We can't breathe! Enough!"

"Yeah, no one's farting. That's something," William said.

He nodded, then shrugged, then looked out the window, his eyes covered by the black wraparound sunglasses he used for climbing. And in that moment I knew he was gone.

"Want me to read some more *Penthouse Forum*?" I said. "There's a thing about a guy who's having sex with twin sisters who later have sex with each other in front of—"

"No, that's okay," he interrupted.

I rummaged through my carry-on bag, looking for something else that might cheer William up. I thought I had some of that watermelon gum he liked. Instead, I came upon the gift I had gotten for William's father. I knew his father liked to draw, and so my sister and I had gone to an art supply store, picking out a special kit for him with a set of creamy pastels, rows of pencils, and a small palette of watercolors, as well as a heavy pad. I remember trying to hide the art supplies in my carry-on, burying them under a copy of *Vanity Fair,* as if seeing them would somehow remind William that his father was dead. I just didn't want him to see anything that might make him feel worse.

An hour later William and I silently ate the meat tamales his mother had given us and picked at slices of his sister's delicate lemon cake. I knew I was desperate when I noticed William staring down at his empty cup. "You need a Coke?" I said. "You stay there! I'll get you a Coke! I'll go get a Coke!" At which point I proceeded to hunt down the stewardess as if she were an elephant in an Ernest Hemingway story.

WHEN WE GOT back to Manhattan, the phone rang constantly, with people offering congratulations. My cousin called and said, "Oh my God. Amy Cohen is getting married! It gives me hope it could happen for me. Is William so excited? Are you guys so happy? You must be ecstatic."

"I can't talk right now," I whispered, explaining that William was in the other room, sitting silently, staring at the ceiling.

"You have to call me later," she said. "We need to talk about your dress and your shower. And I know this amazing photographer you could use, he usually does magazine work and rock stars, but he does weddings too, but you have to book him early. And you know you really have to think about place settings, and the invitations have to go out if it's in May and . . ."

As she continued talking, I tiptoed into my bedroom to check on my silent boyfriend. Usually he was lying on his back, in the dark, wide awake, sighing. It reminded me of how we'd looked when we'd told each other all those stories about our former relationships. Just us, lying on the bed, staring at the ceiling, comparing our pasts and imagining our future.

When the woman from City Bakery called to tell me about catering menus and that the date we'd requested was in fact free—which was a miracle, she added—I whispered that I had to call her back. It was the same with the guy who phoned to suggest deejays for the reception. The man I'd been calling for weeks. William maintained he still wanted to get married in May, but I wasn't so sure it was the best idea now. His family was in shock. His father's presence was very much alive in the house, his clothes and books remaining as they'd always been.

And also, I was starting to feel like an idiot even bringing up the topic of our wedding. There were incidents like the time I said to William, "My family wants to have an engagement party for us, nothing big or fancy, just something with the family, maybe at my sister's, dinner and dessert. She called to ask if we could give her a date, so she can start preparing and inviting people." It was only after I'd finished that I noticed William's eyes were glassy.

"I just cannot fucking believe he's gone," he said. "Gone. Like that."

. . .

AND SOON I started to feel as if we barely knew each other. We were like one of those Indian couples in an arranged marriage, the relative strangers who are promised to each other and then begin the process of finding out if they can get along. I thought about how fitting it was that William was an ice climber, because I felt as if these days I was constantly trying to scale the ice that encased him, to find a way over and around it, usually unsuccessfully.

William now said things like "This is why I was going to cancel our first date. I shouldn't have called you when I knew my dad was dying, because I knew this would happen and this isn't fair to you. I mean, if you had known all this shit was going to happen, would you have said yes to that first date?"

And then I would launch into a whole speech, peppered with things like "This is life and love." And "This is what relationships are really about. It's not about trips and everything being easy." And I went on, and on, and after a few sentences I don't think either one of us was listening anymore.

William told me that once while he was teaching *Antigone,* he said, "Irony is the great gift to tragedy." I loved that quote and remembered it now, because of the irony in our tragedy, namely that the only thing that seemed to make him feel any better these days was my cooking. I mention irony because, for years, I'd desperately and achingly wanted to be a cook, but after age thirty-seven I thought, "If it hasn't happened by now it's probably too late to learn." Throughout my life, whether I tried to make an easy lasagna or even a simple herbed omelette, it seemed as if everything I cooked became a reason to stock up on steel wool. Or new pans. I was used to phrases like "It's just the smoke alarm again!" and "I'm sorry. I thought chicken was supposed to be bright pink in the middle." I had no idea how long to cook a hard-boiled egg. But I was wrong about my chances being over.

A week after we met, when I found out William had been eating hippie cereals and canned tuna fish for dinner, I set out to win him with home-cooked meals. I started by watching the Food Network the way young children watch cartoons, sitting so close to the television I could have gotten a tan. I studied the stirring and the boiling until I could finally understand the skill involved in dumping boxed spaghetti in water and adding canned sauce. From there I moved on to more ambitious things: baked turkey meatballs, marinated chicken on the Foreman grill, halibut roasted in foil. And then I basically went crazy. Chicken Piccata, which needed to be whisked right at its peak; rice pudding, which involved so much stirring I practically got carpal tunnel; homemade hummus and finely chopped tabouli; and my greatest accomplishment—a balsamic roast chicken stuffed with oranges and lemons. I was on a mission. I could now look at a cookbook with a certain amount of confidence. Before I always felt like one of those adults who'd been illiterate their whole lives and said when they tried to read the newspaper they just saw scrambled letters. That's how I'd always felt looking at cookbooks, but not anymore. And so, every night I tried to prepare something for William that he loved.

The poor man. I e-mailed him questions about whether he wanted Greek shrimp with feta or the soba noodle salad with the tangy soy dressing, and did he want the oatmeal chocolate chip cookies? After three weeks of this, he looked down at his belly one night after dinner.

"Oh great," he said. "My dad's dead and now I'm getting fat."

SOON WE BEGAN to bicker. And ultimately, the bickering turned to fights, the first one having to do with moving in together. I loved William's Brooklyn studio; I had often described it as the apartment of an older Latino jazz musician. There were imposing John Coltrane posters and ethnic rugs, as well as a massive bookcase, which held William's collection of first edition books. The whole atmosphere said, "Chill, cat. The world can wait." But my apartment could not have been more different. I have a white circular table that looks as if it could be used for a dinner party on Pluto. My bedroom walls are lavender and my office is a startling shade of hot pink. William asked where we would put his massive bookcase. "In storage?" I suggested hopefully.

I'd forgotten how scary it was to fight with a boyfriend. How my stomach felt as if it were coiling around itself and might eventually explode as I explained that our furniture clashed. Didn't he agree? I forgot you're not supposed to use phrases like "You make me feel as if" or "Why are you going insane?" because it's attacking the other person. When I told this to Eve, she said, "But you're so much better at fighting than I am. You're so sweet. I always start with 'Listen, you limited fuck!' " I forgot at moments that William's father had just died and that I should give the guy a break, even if he was saying my furniture was cold and trendy.

When I told my father we'd gotten engaged, he said, "But have you had a fight yet?" And I said no. And he said, "Well, that worries me." Now, as William and I began to argue more and more, I thought of telling my father, "Well, there's some good news."

Our fights were even more terrifying because we'd made our relationship so public. I knew there were people who thought William and I weren't going to last. I knew this because someone had said, "If this were anyone else I'd be convinced there was no way in hell you two would make it down the aisle." Other people were now asking if I was pregnant. "No?" one of them said. "Wow. I'm shocked. I assumed that's why you two rushed into this." Now if William or I said, "That's it!" or "I'm leaving," we'd have to tell our entire world we hadn't worked out after all.

I started to think that even when things were calm between us, it was like Loch Ness, where a monster might rise out at any moment. This was around the time William had a dream he was in a rowboat with a baby and an elephant during a storm on rough seas.

"You had a dream about you, a baby, and an elephant?" I said.

"Yeah," he said. "Why?"

William was well aware that, at thirty-nine, I wanted children, and that I didn't have a lot of time before things became more difficult. "Well, clearly the baby is the elephant that's always in our room," I said. "And we're on rough seas."

"That we are," he said.

WILLIAM'S FATHER HAD asked to be cremated, and a memorial service was arranged for March.

"You don't have to go," he said. "I have to go back to California. I need to be with my mom. I'm staying for the week."

"Of course I'm going," I said. "Oh, wait, shit. That Tuesday is my sister's last chemo treatment, we're having champagne; but I'll call her and I know she'll understand."

"Okay, but we're staying with my mother, and you know she's going to make us sleep in separate bedrooms."

"Are you trying to talk me out of this?"

"No, I just feel like it's a lot to ask," he said.

"Well, it's not," I said.

I remembered how when my mother died I'd felt the same way, as if exposing people to the details of my life was too much to ask. As if my answering the question "How are you?" was exposing them to things they preferred not to think about. From my own experience I was well aware that there were people who could deal with death and disease, and many who couldn't, and sometimes you couldn't tell the difference, so it was better not to try. There were people who said, "I'm totally here for you. Anything. Just ask," and then you would ask and they'd get a pained look on their face, like "Couldn't you have asked anything else?" I didn't want William to think of me that way.

THE MORNING OF the service, we dressed quickly and headed over to the church with William's family. It was crowded, and we heard that several people had driven all night to be there. The priest, who knew William's father, spoke first, saying what a generous, warm man he was. Then William's nieces and his brother-in-law spoke. I listened, but I was paying more attention to William, who was holding my hand tightly while staring off into the distance.

After the funeral we took a walk around the block, just the two of us, before we went to the reception to see all the relatives and friends. William was dressed in a loose, dark suit, and I was wearing a short-sleeved, black dress with cap sleeves. My feet were killing me. We took a few more steps and that's when I started crying.

"Why are you crying?" he said. "*I'm* not even crying."

"I don't want this for you," I said. "I wish none of this had happened."

He pulled me into his heavy, wool jacket and I cried onto his collar. I couldn't stop thinking about how blind I'd been. For so many years I'd thought about how much I wanted a relationship, but I never thought about all the shit you endure together. Maybe in an abstract way, but now I understood what my friend meant when she said, "A relationship causes as many problems as it solves." I had believed blindly for all those years that somewhere, someplace, there was someone who, when I would say, "This is my shit. Are you still in? Yes or no?" would stay for the next test and the next test after that. I believed this as blindly as I now believed William and I would stick this out. Are you still in? Yes or no? Do you want to work this out? He might want to throttle me because I was too pushy, and I might want to kill him for whatever reason bothered me at that moment, but I believed we'd always answer yes. I do.

A YEAR PASSED, and we still hadn't gotten married. After a while we didn't even talk about it anymore. For one thing, William hated Manhattan.

"Someone sat on me on the subway this morning," he announced one night, after work. "This huge, sweaty doofus tried to wedge himself into the seat next to me and then he crushed my thigh with his big, sweaty, hairy ass. And I was wearing shorts! And there are just too many fucking people in this fucking city. And it's hot. And it smells."

Then he repeated the question he now asked daily.

"Can't we move to California? We could live so well there. We could have a little house by the beach. You can write anywhere. We could be out in the fresh air and the sun and go biking. You'd love it."

And then I gave my usual response.

"That sounds great. For two weeks. I'm in."

William then repeated his other reason for wanting to leave. A reason I couldn't argue with.

"I need to be closer to my mother. She's a widow now, it's different, and I want to help her with stuff. When I was there I helped her clean out the garage and then I installed her storm windows. She needs me."

I'd long said that my ideal arrangement would be something bicoastal—like Oprah or Sweden's royal family, traveling with a small but dedicated staff and private plane. But neither of us could afford two rents, and I wasn't ready to leave Manhattan completely. Although my sister had been given a clean bill of health, I found myself wanting to keep her as close to me as possible. I delighted in her every move, like a mother studying her newborn. I was eager to sit and watch her as she ate brown rice sushi or tried on yet another pair of suede loafers. The rest of my family was in New York. All my friends. This was reason enough to stay in Manhattan. But William and I both knew the truth. There were other things.

It seemed that every argument we had, every disagreement about where to live or how organic chicken was straining our grocery budget, led to his saying, again, "I'm not ready to have a baby."

I'd fantasized about having children long before I ever considered whom I might have them with. Depending on the year, the names and locations changed, but never my desire to have a family. In my late twenties, when I was a struggling screenwriter living in Los Angeles, there were Felix and Liesl, who I was determined to keep "Un-Hollywood." (In my fantasy, my children coincided with my Oscar nomination.) In my thirties, I tended toward names like Gigi and Bebe, names that would ensure that my daughters would grow up to be hookers or, with any luck, high-class hookers. In my late thirties there was Daisy, whom I'd either adopted from China or conceived with a sperm donor. Like my own mother, I'd keep her up watching old movies, offering trivia like "Mae West was the original choice to play Norma Desmond." And while these fantasies shifted, the reality was that, at thirty-nine, I had waited much longer than I'd ever imagined.

William told me that he never thought about having children until he met me. "It was never something I wanted," he explained. "But now, with you, I think I might be ready, one day, but not yet."

"Okay. Well, when?" I said.

He thought for a moment. "Like in five years."

"In five years?" I said. "In five years I'll be seventy!"

WE TRIED TO kid about our standoff. As we were walking past a stylish maternity boutique on Madison Avenue, the kind for women whose stomachs were smaller than mine well into their eighth month, William put his hand over my eyes and said, "Don't look! Just keep walking." We also had a running joke that if I ever decided to adopt, I was going to say that I had plenty of experience with my older, Mexican son.

Then there was the time William showed me a short story he was working on. In the first scene, a teacher goes home to find out that his girlfriend left him because he didn't want to have a baby.

I started laughing.

"Um, okay, and you call this fiction?"

"It is," he said.

I pointed out that the description of the girlfriend was eerily similar to my own.

"That's not true," he said, pointing to my newly highlighted blond hair. "For one thing, the girlfriend in the story's a brunette."

"Yeah, well, wait until my roots grow in."

I STARTED TO imagine just how much I would resent William if, after five years, I couldn't have a child, and how angry I would be at myself if I never tried. I'd heard stories about men who didn't want children, but then became doting fathers, but I'd heard just as many about men who felt trapped and resented their new role.

One night at dinner, William told me a story about a couple he knew. "They went through, like, thirty thousand dollars on in-vitro and then they finally had a kid and the kid has all these allergies, and now they're broke paying for all the medical bills, and they both have to work two jobs, so they never even see the kid."

"I think it's worth it," I said.

"Dogs," he said, pointing his finger in my direction. "They're cute. They're fun. They love you unconditionally. Think about it: dogs. That's the way to go."

MORE AND MORE, while I couldn't imagine being apart, I couldn't imagine how we were ever going to stay together.

I wondered if we should break up, but the thought terrified me. I knew that you could love someone and still have things not work out, but could I really give this up? We still had so much fun together; that is, when we weren't talking about anything that had to do with the rest of our lives.

"If I were twenty-two, this would be the perfect relationship," I told my sister.

I remembered my last breakup: the marathon weeping; the colossal anxiety and dry-cornflake eating; the rash that, on a good day, once made a small child run away crying. I was determined to do anything to avoid going through that pain. Adding to my anxiety was the swell of nausea that accompanied the thought of dating again. The uncomfortable phone calls. The first time he saw me naked. The wondering why he never called again. I didn't have the stomach for it. I still loved William. I could make this relationship work. I was sure of it. I just had to try harder.

And I did.

I cooked our favorite meals, which now included a sautéed

chicken stuffed with minced prosciutto and a vegetable casserole of cauliflower, yams, and portobello mushrooms baked in garlic oil and layers of Parmesan cheese. I rarely saw my other friends, preferring to stay home with William and do Gregory Peck imitations as we watched *The Omen*. I started work on a romantic comedy about a couple whose relationship is in serious trouble and who, in spite of overwhelming odds, work everything out. My plan was that if it sold, we could move back to Los Angeles. I came to feel that I was entirely responsible for making things work and even more responsible if they didn't.

"How's my favorite Stepford Wife?" Eve asked one day when she called.

"Exhausted," I said.

IN EARLY SPRING, William quit his job. He was tired of private school politics and parents who called on weekends to complain when their children got B's. He was going to focus on writing a book, and the idea of this new start made California even more appealing.

"I don't want you to even mention having kids for six months. I can't talk about kids because I need to focus on work and I want us to move to California."

"Are you giving me an ultimatum?" I asked.

He thought about it.

"I guess," he said. "Sorta."

And then I said something that surprised us both, as if a third person in the room, a stranger, had spoken.

"Then go," I said.

William bought his plane ticket, and then the next week, the movers came, loading more than fifty boxes into their truck.

There would be no wedding, no life together. I'd have to tell everyone they were right: we rushed into it too fast. While forty days seemed like an eternity to be stuck in an ark with a bunch of smelly, mating animals, apparently it wasn't long enough to sustain our relationship. And while Noah endured forty days of torrential rains, I now tortured myself with a flood of happy memories: the time William and I went sledding and were too cold to undress so we got into bed with ice caked on our jeans. Our trip to the Grand Canyon, which we called the "Grand Panic Attack," because I was so terrified of heights that I preferred to see the grandeur of the canyon from the parking lot. Or better yet, on a postcard. The time William got a heavy, winter coat at a thrift store and we realized after a month that it was actually a ladies' coat.

Now William was the one finding me sitting in the dark, sighing.

"It kills me to see you like this," William said, crawling next to me.

"I'm worried this is just the beginning," I said, crying.

And soon the morning came when, dressed in his favorite white linen "Jesus" shirt, dark jeans, and all his many necklaces, William went back to California.

. . .

THAT DAY, AS if I were waiting for a package to arrive, I waited to fall apart. I had long considered myself the emotional equivalent of a cheap piñata; one blow and everything—all the knickknacks and detritus—would come pouring out. I'd wilted when even brief relationships didn't work out, crumbled when jobs fell through.

I remember thinking that my dermatologist said it best. On a visit shortly after my rash had started clearing up, I'd asked whether my skin was dry or oily.

"Neither," Dr. Navasky said, looking at the few red bumps that remained. "You're very sensitive. With thin skin."

"Oh, yes, I am." I laughed. "That's so perfect."

When I still hadn't cried the day after William left, I figured it was only because I was so tired from staying awake the night before together, watching *The Omen* yet again and saying things like, "I'm going to miss your skinny wrists and all those fucking bracelets."

After a few days, I was positive I was in denial. I was sad, but I was functioning—eating, sleeping—which was so unlike me. The enormity of my situation—the end of the only real relationship I'd had in six years, the boyfriend I loved so much, the reality of being on my own again at age forty, would, I was sure, sooner or later, eat me alive. That was who I was. Wasn't it?

My phone rang nonstop. I was convinced everyone just wanted to make sure I didn't have my head in the oven—yet.

Eve. My sister. My father. His girlfriend, Beverly. My brother. My doorman.

"How are you?" they all asked, concerned.

"I'm okay," I said.

There was a long pause, as they wondered if they had gotten the wrong number.

"I mean, I'm not great. I'm sad, but I'm actually okay. I can't explain it either."

That I might somehow feel stronger after breaking up with the only man I'd ever been engaged to was something I never would have thought possible. It still felt like an out-of-body experience, not to be at least craving antianxiety medication. After a month, I started to wonder if maybe it was never too late to become a not-total-basket-case. To become stable, tough even, while working toward ballsy.

"I never imagined you as the 'happily ever after' type," one friend told me.

Noticing my alarm, she corrected herself.

"Wait, that came out wrong. I mean, not like the cookie-cutter 'I just need to be married no matter what' happily-ever-after type."

"That's so funny," I said. "Because I thought that's all I ever wanted."

Maybe, after all these years, I finally understood what my mother meant when she said, "People who want to be married are married." She assured me I'd ultimately come to my own conclusion and I had. And it only took me fifteen years. I could have been married. I could have said yes to all those things, and my only solace now was telling myself, "Not at any price." This was my shit. For better or worse.

I didn't say it out loud, for fear that people would think I was a few weeks shy of toting magical crystals and quoting from the I Ching, but I'd started to feel that even though I'd lost my ice climber, I was now scaling the snowy mountain myself. I wouldn't be getting married. I might never get married. I wasn't even sure I wanted to get married anymore. But in the same way I never would have imagined that at thirty-five I'd learn to ride a bike, or that I'd ever be able to roast a chicken, or not completely fall apart after the devastating end to my only engagement, now I knew that anything was possible. I knew this in a way I never had. So much, in fact, that I could now answer the question "Do you think you'll be okay?" with a confident "I do."